A WALKING TOUR

of the

GEORGETOWN SET

The golden dome at the corner of Wisconsin Avenue and M Street gleams in the sunset.

A WALKING TOUR

of the

GEORGETOWN SET

RICK MASSIMO

Photography by Missy Janes

Guilford, Connecticut

An imprint of Rowman & Littlefield

Distributed by NATIONAL BOOK NETWORK

British Library Cataloguing in Publication Information Available

Library of Congress Cataloging-in-Publication Data
Names: Massimo, Richard, 1964–
Title: A walking tour of the Georgetown set / Rick Massimo ; photographs by Missy Janes.
Description: Guilford, Connecticut : Lyons Press, 2016.
Identifiers: LCCN 2016007523 (print) | LCCN 2016009331 (ebook) | ISBN 9781442251069 (hardcover : alkaline paper) | ISBN 9781442251083 (electronic)
Subjects: LCSH: Georgetown (Washington, D.C.)—Tours. | Washington (D.C.)—Tours. | Politicians—Homes and haunts—Washington (D.C.)—Guidebooks. | Celebrities—Homes and haunts—Washington (D.C.)—Guidebooks. | Dwellings—Washington (D.C.)—Guidebooks. | Historic buildings—Washington (D.C.)—Guidebooks. | Walking—Washington (D.C.)—Guidebooks. | Politicians—United States—Biography—Miscellanea. | Celebrities—Washington (D.C.)—Biography—Miscellanea.
Classification: LCC F202.G3 M37 2016 (print) | LCC F202.G3 (ebook) | DDC 917.5304—dc23
LC record available at http://lccn.loc.gov/2016007523

♾™ The paper used in this publication meets the minimum requirements of American National Standard for Information Sciences—Permanence of Paper for Printed Library Materials, ANSI/NISO Z39.48-1992.

CONTENTS

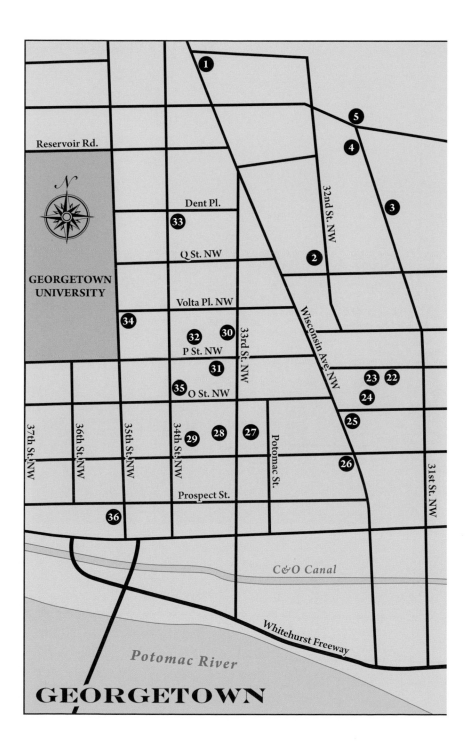

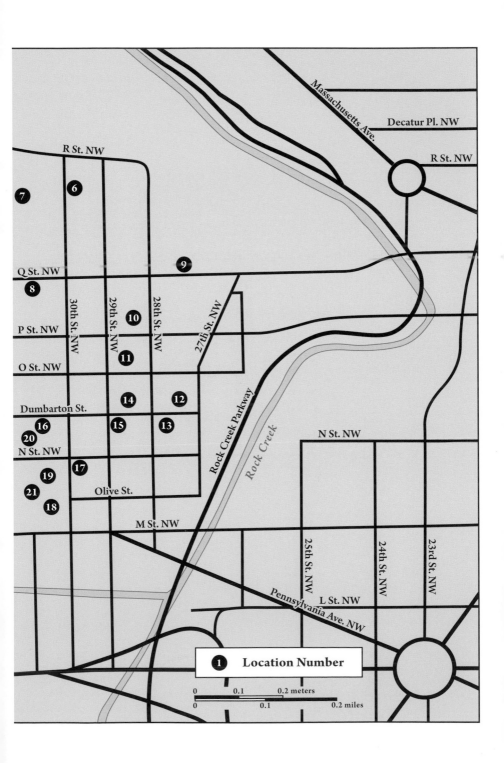

INTRODUCTION

Georgetown, one of Washington's most exclusive neighborhoods, has borne witness to critical moments in American history ever since the Colonial era, but the Cold War history of the area particularly lends itself to a walking tour. For the bureaucratic, journalistic, and diplomatic elite of the era, known as the Georgetown Set, the houses pictured here weren't just a place to hang one's hat in between marathon days at the office. The parties, dinners, and cocktail gatherings held here were the sites of momentous decisions, crafty intrigues, and whispered disclosures—and, hanging in the balance, the denizens of Georgetown thought, not without some justification, was the fate of the world. As Henry Kissinger famously said, "The hand that mixes the Georgetown martini is time and again the hand that guides the destiny of the Western world."

Frank George Wisner, a son of one of the figures profiled in these pages, once said, "One notable feature about Washington at that time is that there wasn't anything to do. . . . Essentially, for dinner and conversation, you moved around from house to house." The Georgetown party of these years wasn't just a place to let your hair down. It was a place to keep, or improve, your place in the pecking order, to make alliances, to gather information. And the powerful gathered to continue the conversations that had gone on in the office. While these days the name of the game seems to be to give journalists as little meaningful information as possible, back then they were easily included in these conversations, and were often openly lobbied for their support of major initiatives such as the Marshall Plan and the Korean War. Meanwhile, as mice scurry between the hooves of elephants, spies from many nations—including the United States—trolled the halls of these houses during festive affairs, looking for hints.

Products by and large of America's finest boarding schools (such as Groton and Andover) and universities (Harvard and Yale, with an occasional Princeton man thrown in for variety), those who lived in these houses took on the challenge of determining the United States' place in the post–World War II world. The people who lived here were not, for the most part, elected officials. They didn't have election-speech promises to keep. They worked as they pleased for the goals they thought best served the nation. Indeed, a couple of them were openly contemptuous of the idea that mere voters should influence their decisions. They saw themselves as doing the dirty work for a great cause.

Some thought war with the Soviet Union was inevitable, and the nation did come perilously close to a declaration a few times. Others foresaw the partition of Europe. Either way, they almost unanimously saw the United States as the superpower that not only could, but should, remake as much of the world as possible in its image.

"Some have argued that the fundamental assumptions of this American Century were flawed from the beginning," Robert Merry writes in his biography of Joe and Stewart Alsop, the journalistic brothers whose approval presidents coveted and whose uncanny access they often cursed. "World peace, according to this view, did not depend on American intrusion into the affairs of struggling nations, did not require the global competition with Soviet Russia that left America so overextended and despised throughout the world. Perhaps not. But this misses the essential point about the nation and its elite—that they were only fulfilling their destiny as determined by generations of training and influence. One might just as well argue that it was unnecessary for the Romans to build their empire. They built it precisely because they were Romans. The American nation, in creating the American Century, was propelled by similar mysterious impulses."

In these pages you'll read about how close the United States came to full-on war with the Soviets, about men who were tormented by their own demons, accented by the stress and world-changing stakes of their jobs, until they took their own lives. You'll also read about the time an international incident was avoided by the intentional tipping over of a tea set, and the time another was begun by crawling through a bathroom window.

Georgetown's iconic Key Bridge.

The houses of the powerful in Georgetown were, by and large, not fancy ones. They didn't need to be. The power wielded behind these walls didn't need to announce itself, and it was all the more powerful for that. To walk the sidewalks of this neighborhood where a Supreme Court justice and a secretary of state would walk to work together, where CIA operatives and powerful publishers would stumble home after a few drinks together, is to walk in their footsteps, if only for a few hours.

1

LA NIÇOISE (NOW CASBAH CAFÉ)
1721 WISCONSIN AVENUE

*T*he building that now houses the Casbah Café was in the 1950s the restaurant La Niçoise, where waiters on roller skates delivered French food and the counterintelligence master of the CIA had a weekly lunch date with a Soviet spy.

In the world of spying, there's intelligence—spying on other people—and counterintelligence—preventing other people from spying on you. James Jesus Angleton was the head of the counterintelligence staff at the CIA from 1954 to 1975 and came here weekly to

The Casbah Café (1721 Wisconsin Avenue) is a Mediterranean place now, but in the 1950s it was a French restaurant where a British spy tricked an American one.

drink, eat, talk, and drink some more with Kim Philby, who officially worked at the British Embassy but was a spy for Britain's MI6 as well as for the KGB.

In 1961 Anatoliy Golitsyn defected from the Soviet Union with a hat-load of knowledge about the inner workings of the KGB as well as the names of several diplomats and spies who were in fact working for Soviet intelligence. One of them was Philby, who was recalled to England and who defected to the Soviet Union in 1963 when the walls finally began to close in on him after about a dozen years of suspicion Angleton ignored.

Between the Golitsyn accusations and the missed opportunity with Philby, Angleton—who had carried out the agency's first dirty-tricks campaign in a foreign country when he was given a $10 million budget to influence the 1948 Italian elections—became obsessed with the idea of "moles" in the CIA. While it may have been reasonable, between the size of the CIA and the formidable Soviet threat, to assume that some infiltration had or was about to happen, many said

Book Hill Park is just a block and a half south of the Casbah Café; take a moment to trek up the hill for beautiful vistas of Georgetown and the Potomac.

that Angleton's "molehunt" hurt as much as it helped: Innocent people were punished; agents and employees were wary about sharing
information; Soviets who made overtures about becoming double
agents were rejected as plants.

On October 12, 1964, Mary Pinchot Meyer, the sister-in-law of
then-*Newsweek* Washington bureau chief Ben Bradlee, was shot to
death on Georgetown's C&O Canal. Bradlee went to her house, where
he was met in the living room by Angleton. Speculation centered on
the likelihood that they were both looking for Mary's diary, as she was
having an affair with JFK. No diary has ever been found.

Angleton was also deeply involved with Operation Chaos and
Operation Mockingbird—the CIA's controversial efforts to spy on the
anti-Vietnam War movement and to set up front groups working in
the American press, respectively. "It is inconceivable," Angleton once
said, "that a secret arm of the government has to comply with all the
overt orders of the government."

When the details of Operation Mockingbird were made public—
or, perhaps, too public to ignore—as part of the uncovering of the
CIA's "Family Jewels," Angleton was forced to resign on Christmas
Eve 1974.

ERIC SEVAREID

1610 32ND STREET

*Y*ou couldn't make up Eric Sevareid.

Born in North Dakota and raised in Minneapolis, Sevareid was working in the Paris bureaus of United Press and the *New York Herald Tribune* when broadcasting pioneer Edward R. Murrow asked him to come to London and try his hand at radio reporting for CBS. Sevareid and the rest of "Murrow's Boys" ended up basically inventing the form in the crucible of World War II.

Sevareid was the first reporter to break the news that France was surrendering to the Nazis in June 1940. He then went to London and along with Murrow covered the Battle of Britain from the very city over which planes were dogfighting and dropping bombs. After a short stint in Washington, Sevareid volunteered to cover the China-Burma-India theater of operations. It's not known what he thought of that decision as the plane he was in plummeted to earth with engine trouble in 1943, but he and the crew survived and walked out of the jungle after nineteen days. He also covered the Italian and southern French campaigns.

After the war his autobiography, *Not So Wild a Dream*, covered his journey from a boyhood spent canoeing and mixing with hoboes to seeing the horrific ending of World War II in Germany, and went through eleven printings over the next twenty-eight years. But he was just getting warmed up for the career that most Americans knew him for.

While he lived in this relatively modest house on the edge of the manicured grounds of Tudor Place, Sevareid continued to report for CBS—heading the Washington bureau from 1946 to 1954, acting as a roving European correspondent from 1959 to 1961, and hosting

Eric Sevareid, who lived here at 1610 32nd Street, was one of "Murrow's Boys" and among the journalists who invented TV news as we know it today.

many news-related series. He also began delivering short commentaries on the issues of the day, first on radio and then on television. On November 22, 1963, Walter Cronkite, in the midst of a multi-hour marathon of live coverage of the assassination of President Kennedy, threw to Sevareid for some information on the future President Johnson. Sevareid deftly and gracefully summed up the man, ending by saying, "the course of the country itself now lies with the continuing nature of our times and of the world itself."

Out of that tragic afternoon, a pattern was set: For the next fourteen years, Cronkite, known as the most trusted man in America, would anchor the *CBS Evening News*, and Sevareid would follow up with analysis that was beautifully written, topical, and wise, delivered in a honeyed, stentorian voice that echoed his years in radio. "Eric was one of that small number of news analysts, commentators and essayists who truly deserve to be called distinguished," Cronkite later said. "A philosopher, writer, reporter and teacher, with no equal in the history of broadcast journalism," Cronkite's successor, Dan Rather, added.

Eric Sevareid's final commentary aired in 1977, though he continued to appear on the network in various capacities. "There is in the American people a tough, undiminished instinct for what is fair," he said in his signoff. "Rightly or wrongly, I have the feeling that I have passed that test. I shall wear this like a medal." His final televised appearance was in 1991; he died the following year.

"It was a lucky stroke of timing to have been born and to have lived as an American in this last generation," Sevareid wrote in the 1976 edition of *Not So Wild a Dream*. "It was good fortune to be a journalist in Washington, now the greatest single news headquarters in the world since ancient Rome."

3

AL FRIENDLY

1645 31ST STREET

*A*l Friendly is probably best known for the job he lost: He was managing editor of the *Washington Post* from 1955 until the legendary Ben Bradlee took over in 1965. But those who knew him say he served in that post with grace in a difficult time, and without question he fashioned himself a second act in life.

Born in Salt Lake City, Friendly worked briefly in the Department of Commerce before coming to the *Post* in 1939 as a reporter. He was in army intelligence during World War II and wrote the book *The Guys on the Ground*. In 1947 he spent the summer with *Post* owner and publisher Eugene Meyer inspecting and documenting conditions on the war-destroyed European continent in preparation for the push by Congress to approve the massive foreign-aid package that came to be known as the Marshall Plan. "We were Marshall Plan even before Marshall," Friendly would later say.

Friendly then worked for Averell Harriman as press officer in the Marshall Plan office in Paris, generating coverage of the results of the aid package. When he returned to the *Post*, he covered topics including atomic energy, the debate in the Truman administration over whether to develop the hydrogen bomb, and the beginnings of Senator Joe McCarthy's witch hunt of suspected communists in the US government.

In 1952 publisher Phil Graham, who knew Friendly from the army, made him assistant managing editor of the *Post*. He advanced to the managing editor's job in 1955. It was a time of great growth for the newspaper, which had recently acquired the *Washington Times-Herald*, but there were other challenges. Ben Bradlee wrote in his memoir that, particularly later in Friendly's tenure as managing editor,

He may have gotten pushed out of his biggest job, but Al Friendly ended his career exactly the way he wanted to—and he did better in his second act than his first.

the effects of Phil Graham's mental problems made running the paper more difficult than it had to be. Many managers, including Friendly, "were fired, then rehired. Many were confronted with decisions taken by Phil—a new bureau here, a new executive there—pursuant to priorities and policies that were at least erratic. . . . The men who held the paper together [including Friendly, Bradlee remembered] made all future progress possible, and I knew it, and they knew I knew it."

The haste with which Bradlee unseated Friendly as managing editor—scarcely three months after coming to the *Post* from *Newsweek*—appeared a little unseemly, particularly since Friendly had spent so much time visiting Graham during his hospitalizations. And, when a distraught Katharine Graham, Meyer's daughter, took over the *Post* after her husband's suicide and asked rhetorically, "What am I going to do now?" Friendly simply replied, "You're going to run the joint." The idea evidently hadn't occurred to anyone, but it began a publishing career for Katharine Graham that was just as legendary as her husband's.

Bradlee, however, says the change at the *Post* was all for the best. Friendly, he writes, "appeared to me from Day One as miscast in the role of managing editor, the job on a daily newspaper where all the thousand details of administration and production have to be coordinated before the paper can be in a position to write the great stories." While Bradlee was hardly a neutral observer to the situation, Friendly's post-managing-editor career certainly provided at least some confirming evidence.

While many in Friendly's shoes would stomp out of the news-room never to be heard from again, with perhaps a few choice words in the doorway, Friendly stayed with the *Washington Post* on the "new ideas" beat—one he invented himself—and wrote as a foreign correspondent and chief of the *Post*'s London bureau. He won a Pulitzer Prize in 1967 for his reporting on the Six-Day War in Israel.

Meanwhile, his wife, Jean, played a critical role in holding George-town society together: She was the head of the Wives' Protection Club, meaning she would keep an eye on the husbands during the summer, when they were left alone in Washington as their families vacationed. Jean's sister was married to another prominent Wash-ington powerbroker, James H. Rowe Jr., who had been a member of FDR's "kitchen cabinet."

Al Friendly had always said that he would retire on his sixtieth birthday, and when it came in 1971, he did. He died here in 1983. This house, across the street from historic Tudor Place (which was first lived in by Martha Washington's granddaughter and which still hosts tours of the house and gardens), has been one of DC's most desired houses: Whenever it has been sold since Friendly's death, it has been for one of the highest prices in the city's history. In 2014, it sold for $16.1 million.

ROBERT TAFT

1688 31ST STREET

*T*he son of former president and Supreme Court chief justice William Howard Taft, Ohioan Robert Taft served in the US Senate from 1939 until his death in 1953 and was known as "Mr. Republican," possibly the best known and most powerful conservative of his time.

As such, he was against much of the New Deal; opposed the United States' entry into World War II (until Pearl Harbor, at least); and, in fact, was against American participation in the Lend-Lease Act, fearing it would ensnare the nation in Europe's war when even many of his fellow conservatives considered aiding England the country's best chance of avoiding the conflict. He also spoke strongly against the internment of Japanese-Americans during the war, a noble if ultimately unsuccessful stand.

He ran for president in 1940, 1948, and 1952, though he never got the party's nomination, losing in 1952 to General Dwight D. Eisenhower after a long, bitter fight that ended only on the convention floor. Indeed, in the context of the globe-spanning American colossus that was built after the Second World War—for that matter, the society that was built at home as well—the thing that stands out most about Senator Robert Taft's career is the number of disputes and conflicts that saw him on the losing end.

After World War II, Taft was a staunch opponent of American involvement in foreign affairs, including such multinational arrangements as NATO, a stand that inspired Eisenhower to run for president in the first place. He was also originally against the Marshall Plan, calling it "a TVA [Tennessee Valley Authority] for Europe"—which in many ways it was, though that characterization isn't immediately

Senator Robert Taft may have lost a lot of battles while he lived here at 1688 31st Street, but the legacy of "Mr. Republican" continued for decades.

pejorative. In the end he voted for the plan, however, as the global situation in 1948 had gotten more dangerous—communists took over Czechoslovakia, overthrowing the only democratic government in Eastern Europe to survive the war, and made gains in Italy and France. Taft was an early supporter of Senator Joe McCarthy's hunt for supposed communists in the US government, though he was willing to actually look at the FBI file of Chip Bohlen during the hearings to confirm him as ambassador to the Soviet Union and rebuke McCarthy's offensive when he saw the facts.

In 1953, after Eisenhower had gone on to win the presidential election, Taft spoke out against involvement in the growing conflicts in Southeast Asia. He presciently warned, "I have never felt that we should send American soldiers to the Continent of Asia, which, of course, included China proper and Indo-China, simply because we are so outnumbered in fighting a land war on the Continent of Asia that it would bring about complete exhaustion even if we were able to win." Interventionists and internationalists such as Joe and Stewart Alsop disagreed with Taft and thought his isolationism dangerous, writing that whatever Taft's motivation, he and his cohorts were voting "the straight communist party line, as laid down by the 'Daily Worker.'" Still, the Alsops respected him, even liked him: A biographer of the brothers writes that Stewart Alsop, upon returning from a talk with Taft, would need a "de-brainwashing" from Joe before starting to write.

While Taft was often perceived as cold and uncaring for some of his policy views, particularly against social programs such as the New Deal, when his wife, Martha, suffered a stroke in 1949, he took care of her personally, even helping to feed her.

After their rancorous presidential primary battle, Taft and Eisenhower mended their relationship, and Taft, thanks to a new GOP majority, got the title of Senate Majority Leader as a consolation prize. He took over in January 1953, but didn't get to enjoy it long. He began to feel pain in his hips soon after, and following a painful golf game with Eisenhower that April, he was diagnosed with pancreatic cancer. He resigned as majority leader that June, and died on July 31.

His family legacy endured: Son Robert Taft Jr. also represented Ohio in the US Senate, and one of his grandsons was elected governor of Ohio in 1998. On Constitution Avenue, near the US Capitol, a

one-hundred-foot monument to Taft, including a ten-foot statue of the former senator, was unveiled in 1959. Bells ring on the hour and quarter hour, and according to the inscription, the monument "stands as a tribute to the honesty, indomitable courage, and high principles of free government symbolized by his life."

5

DUMBARTON OAKS
1703 32ND STREET

*T*he gardens at Dumbarton Oaks, which took former owner Mildred Bliss and landscape gardener Beatrice Farrand nearly thirty years to design and complete, run from terraced gardens to tennis courts to near-wilderness. The grand house itself, the first part of which was built in 1801 on the original land grant that eventually became the formerly independent city of Georgetown, houses a research library affiliated with Harvard University. Legendary events have been held here, but none more so than the Dumbarton Oaks Conference.

By October 1944 the Allied powers—the United States, Great Britain, and the Soviet Union—had Germany and Japan on the run. Of course, nearly a year of war would still devastate Europe and Asia, but the tide had unmistakably turned, and it was time to begin planning what a postwar world would look like.

The Allies had already decided at a conference in Moscow the previous year that as soon as possible, an international organization for the keeping and preservation of peace would be formed—a successor to the post–World War I League of Nations, proposed and brought about by President Woodrow Wilson. But that was an aspirational goal. At a conference held in the mansion on this grand estate, the powers began to get down to the work of what a United Nations—the name already officially chosen by the Allied powers—would look like.

At Dumbarton Oaks, the leaders of the United States, United Kingdom, Soviet Union, and China set forth not only the general notion of the United Nations, but how it would be structured. The Proposals for the Establishment of a General International Organization, which was hammered out here, first laid down on paper the

Dumbarton Oaks is a natural jewel of DC, but attendees at the conference that bears its name had matters aside from the landscape on their minds.

concept of a General Assembly of member nations as well as a Security Council of eleven members, with permanent membership going to the Big Four plus France. Most Security Council matters would require seven affirmative votes, including those of all five permanent members. This basic structure continues today.

In the short documentary *Now—The Peace*, narrator Lorne Greene, at his stentorian best, explained how negotiators at Dumbarton Oaks (the American representative was Undersecretary of State

Edward Stettinius Jr., who would become secretary of state before the year was out and eventually was the first American delegate to the UN) had learned from the mistakes of the League of Nations. Most important among these was the ability of the UN to raise its own peacekeeping force from member nations in order to enforce its resolutions and stop aggressors. The Proposals also included what the documentary called a recognition of "the need to take action before the war clouds break"—a reference not only to the run-up to World War II but the Spanish Civil War, which began in 1936 and was largely ignored by the League of Nations, which considered it an internal matter, ignoring the fact that Germany and Italy were using it as a training ground for troops and tactics they'd be using in Europe and Ethiopia, respectively, in the next few years.

The Dumbarton negotiators also made provisions for what the Proposals called "international cooperation in the solution of international economic, social and other humanitarian problems," recognizing that economic stability and the alleviation of poverty were critical to the governmental stability that keeps the peace. Organizations such as the UN Relief Agency eventually sprung from this notion.

To be sure, there were still kinks to be worked out. The San Francisco Conference of 1945 laid out the final structure of the UN, and at Dumbarton the Soviet Union certainly tried to work their will on the structure. Charles Bohlen, a part of the US delegation and later ambassador to Moscow, noted that the USSR wanted all sixteen Soviet republics to be individual members of the UN, though the idea that each one would truly be free to vote as they liked was already laughable. The conference also had to be split into two phases because the USSR refused to meet face-to-face with China.

Still, before World War II was even over, the process had begun to prevent World War III from happening. Among other things, it was for good or ill the death knell for the kind of American isolationism that had preceded the United States' entry into the ongoing war.

The gardens of Dumbarton Oaks are open to the public. In the winter months, admission is free. Next door is Montrose Park, a large public park overseen by the National Park Service.

6

WILLIAM DONOVAN / PHIL AND KATHARINE GRAHAM

2920 R STREET

William Donovan

*B*ill Donovan said he hated the nickname "Wild Bill," but his wife later said he secretly loved it. Judging from his life and career, his wife's account is far more plausible. Of all Donovan's distinctions, the most far-reaching was his tenure during World War II running the Office of Strategic Services (OSS)—the United States' first national intelligence agency and the forerunner of the CIA. He essentially invented the modern version of spying and covert actions in America.

The son of a railroad superintendent from Buffalo, Donovan fought in World War I, earning the Congressional Medal of Honor. (In his life, he also was awarded the Distinguished Service Cross, the Distinguished Service Medal, and the National Security Medal—the only person to receive all four—as well as the Silver Star and Purple Heart.) He returned to his hometown to become a lawyer and prosecutor, making a lot of enemies after he enforced Prohibition against even the high-society swells who considered themselves above such laws, but he eventually became a deputy assistant to the US attorney general. He left the Justice Department in 1929 and headed to Wall Street, where he worked in private practice, ran unsuccessfully for governor of New York, and traveled the world inveterately on business.

During much of the 1930s, he kept his passport and a bag packed in his office, the better to head off on another trip on short notice. That, plus his good relationship with President Franklin Delano Roosevelt (despite Donovan's being a Republican), made him a valuable

For decades 2920 R Street hosted the kind of Washington party where the real work of running the nation got done.

ear to the ground on the situation in Europe as World War II loomed. A few months before Pearl Harbor, FDR named Donovan coordinator of information as part of the president's efforts to prepare the country for war. At the time each branch of the service, plus the FBI, had its own intelligence agency, and Donovan's job was to straighten out the inefficient mess of that arrangement. He learned from his contacts in England, including Winston Churchill, about the value and the structure of a centralized intelligence service, and in 1942 the OSS was established.

Donovan was a free thinker, with a taste for the good life and the spectacular. His appetite for marital infidelity was massive, and his expensive tastes were legendary—one look at the house on R Street can confirm that. Donovan entertained, held meetings, and sometimes did both at the same time here, earning the OSS the nickname Oh So Social, and he ran the OSS with energy and flair. Not only did Donovan's agency gather intelligence and cultivate sources in foreign countries, it also began to enact covert operations and sabotage on its own. "In a global and totalitarian war," he said, "intelligence must be global and totalitarian."

His assistant, David Bruce, who later became ambassador to France, West Germany, and Great Britain and emissary to China, said that "his imagination was unlimited. Ideas were his plaything. Excitement made him snort like a racehorse. Woe to the officer who turned down a project because, on its face, it seemed ridiculous, or at least unusual." He describes, for example, spending weeks testing the practicality and efficacy of releasing over Tokyo bats with incendiary bombs strapped to their backs.

President Truman broke up the OSS shortly after World War II, in September 1945. He was said to have wanted US intelligence to once again be broken up into smaller units. It's easy to believe he didn't want someone to have the kind of power that Donovan had had.

Donovan agitated for the creation of a similar agency for what so many in and out of intelligence saw as the coming conflict with our former allies in the Soviet Union (and China), and with the passage of the National Security Act of 1947 (the same year he sold this house) creating the Central Intelligence Agency, he got his wish. Donovan never had a formal post in the agency, but four future CIA directors— Allen Dulles, Richard Helms, William Colby, and William Casey—were former OSS men. For good or ill, and often both, his stamp endured.

After the war, Donovan helped prosecute the Nuremberg trials, then returned to private practice. He served a little over a year as ambassador to Thailand, retiring in 1954. He died in 1959.

Phil and Katharine Graham

Katharine Graham's father, Eugene Meyer, bought the *Washington Post* in 1932 at a bankruptcy sale. He began its transformation from the third-best newspaper in Washington to one of the premier papers in the country. After Katharine married Phil Graham in 1940, Eugene offered him a place as his successor as publisher, despite the fact that Graham had no newspaper experience. His own daughter had spent a few years as a reporter in San Francisco. Such was the prevailing sexism of the times.

Phil Graham, however, turned out to be a natural in the news business, investing in and upgrading the reporting staff and making the *Post* a national force for the first time. He worked publicly and behind the scenes for causes such as integration, both nationwide and in DC. A powerful and passionate speaker on the freedom of

the press, he coined the description of journalism as the "first rough draft of history."

Behind his brilliance, however, lay mental and emotional problems that led to a scandalous affair, bizarre public behavior, reputed physical abuse of Katharine, and sometimes months-long absences from work. He committed suicide in 1963, a few months before President Kennedy's assassination. His gravesite is across the street in Oak Hill Cemetery, within easy view of this house. Katharine Graham, also buried there, wrote of the arrangement, "I like this now, but in the beginning it disturbed me a great deal."

She had once said that working for the *Post* would be "a first-class dog's life," but she stepped into the leadership role at the paper and its other businesses, including *Newsweek*. She immediately began learning the ropes. "I suppose that, without quite realizing it, I was taking a veil," she would later write, but it also became clear to those who knew her that she was finding her footing as an independent person. She eventually led the paper through its most tumultuous and most influential period: the late 1960s and 1970s.

The paper took a lead role in the Pentagon Papers case, in which the Nixon administration tried to stop the *Post* and the *New York Times* from publishing stories based on a leaked government history of the Vietnam War (and temporarily succeeded in the case of the *Times*, the only time in American history the Supreme Court stopped publication of a news story). And, of course, two young *Post* reporters named Bob Woodward and Carl Bernstein not only broke the story of the Watergate break-in, but followed the connections to the administration for more than two years, culminating in President Nixon's resignation in 1974.

The administration threw everything it had at the *Post* during the Watergate scandal: Special Counsel Chuck Colson once said publicly, "They're going to wish . . . they'd never heard of Watergate." Moves included an idea to suggest to the *Times* "a butcher piece" on the *Post*'s supposed anti-Nixon agenda and other tactics (references to the "Eastern media elite," objection to the renewal of the company's broadcast licenses) that embattled administrations have hauled out ever since. Katharine Graham, Ben Bradlee, and the rest of the *Post* held firm, despite not even knowing who Woodward and Bernstein's crucial and confidential "Deep Throat" source was.

Attorney General John Mitchell told Bernstein about a Water-gate-related story he was working on, "Katie Graham's gonna get her tit caught in a big fat wringer if that's published." It was published. After Nixon resigned, Bradlee, Woodward, Bernstein, and three other key *Post* staffers gave her a present—an antique laundry wringer.

The house looks like the setting for a grand mansion party from an old movie, and before and after Phil Graham's death, the family kept up the entertaining tradition started by "Wild Bill" Donovan, who lived in the house before the Grahams. Many parties occurred here, including a celebration of Georgetown's 200th anniversary in 1951. Guests included George Kennan, Secretary of State Dean Acheson, House Speaker Sam Rayburn, and Supreme Court Justice Felix Frankfurter. Phil Graham set the tone in a toast rhapsodizing about "the tiny kingdom of Georgetown," where parties "aren't really parties in the true sense of the word. They're business after business hours, a form of government by invitation." He later squared off—physically—with the French ambassador after insulting the country's lack of resolve in Vietnam and extending the insinuation to France's performance in World War II. Katharine Graham, thinking quickly, knocked over the tea tray, distracting everyone from the unpleasant-ness and unconsciously prompting everyone to head for the door as quickly as politeness would allow.

The parties got better from there, and the guest lists only got higher-powered, including presidents, senators, congressmen, jus-tices, and the cream of the media. "You didn't exist unless you'd broken bread with Kay Graham," Evangeline Bruce, no slouch of a hostess herself, once said.

Katharine Graham died in 2001. The guests at the reception after her funeral in Oak Hill Cemetery included Vice President Dick Cheney, former president Bill Clinton and Senator Hillary Rodham Clinton, and Senators Kennedy, Hatch, McCain, and Bob Graham, along with Rupert Murdoch, Arthur Sulzberger, Barbara Walters, Tom Brokaw, Henry Kissinger, Arthur Schlesinger, and dozens more. One guest said, "This is Kay Graham's final party. Kay was known for bringing people together. We've come back to her house today for a last meal and a last chat. She would've loved this party."

WILLIAM COLBY
3028 DENT PLACE

William Colby capped off a career in the shadows as the CIA director who ended up holding the bag.

A product of a New England private-school upbringing, Colby served in the OSS in World War II as a Jedburgh—one of a regiment of paratroopers who would jump behind enemy lines to aid and coordinate with local resistance members. He had missions in France and was particularly lauded for his work in Norway. He went into private law practice after the war, but like so many veterans, couldn't settle back into civilian life.

Colby and his family spent much of the 1950s in Rome, where the work of the CIA, including that of James Angleton, helped stop the spread of communism in Italy. He then went to Saigon, where he was CIA station chief from 1959 to 1961. There, he befriended President Ngo Dinh Diem and his brother Ngo Dinh Nhu, who were killed in a 1963 coup whose planning and execution the United States supported at least tacitly.

By this time, however, Colby was back in Washington, where from this tucked-away house on a quiet side street he acted as the Far East chief for the CIA. He had already tried to re-create his Jedburgh success in Vietnam with Operation Tiger—a spectacular failure in which of 250 South Vietnamese who parachuted into North Vietnam, 217 were killed, captured, or turned into double agents (some of whom were then reportedly killed by the same Americans who had trained and equipped them).

Back in Washington, Colby also instituted the notorious Phoenix Project, which was intended to seize and neutralize the communist Viet Cong infiltration of South Vietnam. What it ended up being was

William Colby, "the man who wasn't there," lived here at 3028 Dent Place.

a program of barbarity carried out by the South Vietnamese, the US military, and the CIA against Vietnamese civilians. "By the time I got there in 1969, it felt much more like an assassination program," Senator Bob Kerrey, a Phoenix Project veteran, told Carl Colby in the latter's documentary about his father, *The Man Who Wasn't There*. At least 26,000 people were killed under the auspices of Phoenix between 1965 and 1972.

"He didn't have a lot of romantic ideas about spying," Carl Colby said about his father. "He saw it for what it was—a dirty business."

William Colby's predecessor, James Schlesinger, undoubtedly felt that in a post-Watergate era of suspicion, some of the illegal and shocking activities of the CIA overseas—and within the United States, where it was explicitly forbidden to operate—were going to be exposed. He put out a call to all CIA employees to send in any record of activities they thought conflicted with the agency's mandated responsibilities. The responses ran to 693 pages and were nicknamed the Family Jewels.

Colby was appointed CIA director under President Nixon and stayed on when Gerald Ford took over, and was in charge when Congress and the public found out about the Family Jewels. He admitted

to *New York Times* journalist Seymour Hersh that illegal wiretapping of Americans had happened, but referred to it as a "skeleton in the closet."

That didn't fly. Colby eventually was called to testify in front of Congress thirty-two times in one year, his son relates, eventually admitting to CIA abuses such as the surveillance of Americans, including journalists; the plan to enlist the Mafia to kill Fidel Castro; the opening of US citizens' mail; the infiltration of the anti–Vietnam War movement; "surreptitious entries" into private properties; and more. While Colby continued to argue with Congress that a certain degree of secrecy was in the national interest, many, including Schlesinger, Ford, and Secretary of State Henry Kissinger, felt he was being too forthcoming as it was. Former national security adviser Brent Scowcroft theorizes in Carl Colby's documentary that Colby, a Catholic, was expiating his guilt: "[He] revealed things that did not have to be revealed."

During Colby's time as CIA director, the Vietnam War ended, and he had to watch as the country collapsed. He argued with Kissinger to make a deal to evacuate from Saigon thousands of Vietnamese who had collaborated with the United States and whose lives would be in danger. In 1976 he resigned and was succeeded by future president George H. W. Bush.

"He was really a tortured soul," Scowcroft says in the documentary. Watergate journalist Bob Woodward says that the job of CIA director required getting "caught between doing the wish[es] of the president, and the law."

This made family life difficult. "Happy was not what his life was about," Carl Colby says. "He was about doing the right thing, about being at the pointy edge of the spear. . . . Among friends he could be relaxed—well, he didn't really have any friends. He had people he worked with."

On the other hand, Colby's other sons, his second wife, and other family members, as well as his biographer Randall Woods, strongly dispute Carl's characterizations. Among these family members, Colby's son John points out that "the Vietnam pacification programs were not a barbarity but part of a thoughtful counterinsurgency program designed to protect and win over, not terrorize, the rural populace of the country. My father had seen the tactics of the Nazi

occupiers in both France and Norway and was implacably opposed to them and saw how they ultimately served to stir up, not subdue the Resistance in both countries."

John Colby also notes his father's openness to Congress was motivated by a combination of idealism and practical political calculation, and that the notion that he took his own life is absurd. He, along with other family members, see Colby as a complicated man with his own share of flaws, but nonetheless a dedicated and deeply principled public servant, a heroic soldier, and an admirable man.

In April 1996 William Colby, who by this time had (despite his Catholicism) divorced and remarried, went out in his canoe. An excellent sailor, he disappeared. The canoe washed up on the banks of the Wicomico River the next day. His body was found nine days later. Naturally, given his career, foul play was suspected, but his son notes that Colby went out in the evening after preparing his favorite meal, and that a picture of his daughter Catherine, who died young from anorexia, was in his wallet when he was found.

8

CYRUS VANCE

hile the most noteworthy chapters in Cyrus Vance's career came later than the historical period we think of as the height of the Cold War, his final act in public life was a rarity in Washington: So many say they're resigning a government post based on principle, but he actually did.

Vance was born in West Virginia but grew up outside New York City, where his father was a lawyer in Manhattan. He died when Cyrus was five years old, and Cyrus became close to his first cousin, lawyer John Davis. (Some reports say Davis adopted Vance.)

After going to Yale, including the law school, and serving in the navy during World War II, Vance was appointed special counsel to the Preparedness Investigating Subcommittee of the Senate Armed Services Committee. It was the beginning of more than twenty years in and out of government service.

An unapologetic member of the Establishment, Vance shared an attitude about the relationship of money and privilege to power with many of his generation: "A lot of us were raised in families where we were taught that we were very fortunate, that we were going to have a good education, and that we had the responsibility to return to the community some of the benefits and blessings we had, and that there was an obligation to participate in government service at the local, state and national level."

His first distinctive achievement, as special counsel, was helping to draw up the legislation establishing NASA in 1958, a post-Sputnik time when space exploration was seen as less an intrepid adventure and more of a matter of national defense.

Vance rose in the ranks of the Defense Department until becoming secretary of the army in 1962, during which time the Cuban

Former secretary of state Cyrus Vance lived here at 3018 Q Street while he was advising President Carter.

Missile Crisis put the army on alert and troops were sent to the University of Mississippi to enforce desegregation. He left for the private sector, but returned as deputy secretary of defense from 1964 to 1967. His negotiating skills were always in demand, however: He was often called back for special assignments, such as helping to defuse a potential Greece-Turkey war and easing tensions in Detroit in the late sixties.

An early supporter of US involvement in Vietnam, Vance turned against the war in later years. He was also a deputy to Averell Harriman at the 1968 Paris peace talks regarding Vietnam, where disagreement over matters such as the shape of the negotiating table famously made the talks difficult. (It has since been learned that the Nixon campaign, with impetus from future national security adviser Henry Kissinger, secretly scuttled the talks by telling the South Vietnamese that the continuation of the war would help bring about a Nixon presidency, and that they'd get a better peace deal under a Nixon administration. The number of people, including American soldiers, who died as a result of this sabotage can't be precisely calculated.)

Vance returned again to private practice, and the boards of various corporations, until 1977, when he was again called to serve as secretary of state in the Carter administration. Vance's personal style and approach to the Soviet Union differed markedly from that of his predecessor, Henry Kissinger. Vance was said to have seen the management of world affairs as no place for an overarching philosophy, seeing instead a necessity to "slog it out" on a situational basis. And while Kissinger was a willing celebrity who mused publicly on such matters as the aphrodisiac qualities of power, Vance was known as "a man who leaves no footprints." Professor Norman A. Graebner, a historian of American diplomacy at the University of Virginia, later said that Vance's positions reflected "the general attitude toward the acceptance of the Soviet position in the world and the fact that revolutionary pressures in the third world were genuine and that it was America's task to live with those realities."

But Vance's most famous act in government service was his last: Disagreeing with President Carter over Operation Eagle Claw, the 1980 mission to rescue the 444 hostages held in Iran, he resigned as secretary of state. He felt the mission was doomed to fail, which

it did. He also believed Carter was being pushed into the mission, largely by national security adviser Zbigniew Brzezinski, after a series of foreign-policy setbacks that his political opponents were using to insinuate that the former navy submarine officer was weak. Critically, Vance resigned before knowing whether he would be proven right. Plenty of government officials resign to distance themselves from failures; the possibility of going along with the majority, and being a part of the reflected glory if it succeeded, didn't enter his mind. Vance was only the second secretary of state to resign over a matter of principle, after William Jennings Bryan in the run-up to US involvement in World War I.

Cyrus Vance died in 2002; he was eighty-four. His son said upon his death, "I don't think he ever failed to follow [his] principles in his entire professional life."

ALLEN DULLES

2723 Q STREET

llen Dulles was the first civilian director of the CIA, and he was instrumental not only in literally creating the agency, but in making it the type of organization it's known as today.

Dulles was in the Foreign Service during World War I and joined the OSS during World War II, working in the Germany operation and eventually running the service's bureau in Switzerland. His achievements included the secret negotiations over the German surrender of Italy. When the war ended, he found returning to his peacetime law firm "an appalling thing" after the tension and excitement of running a spy network. Along with his brother, John Foster Dulles; James Forrestal, the first secretary of defense; and State Department official George Kennan, Dulles formed the Office of Policy Coordination, which operated alongside, and eventually became part of, the CIA.

Dulles laid out to Congress in 1947 the case for an intelligence agency "directed by a relatively small but elite corps of men with a passion for anonymity." Thanks to his work and others', the CIA was created with instructions to gain and distribute intelligence—and to perform "other functions and duties related to intelligence affecting the national security." It's not known how many of those who voted to establish the CIA intended for those "other functions" to include covert operations, the overthrow of governments, and assassination plots, but once the vaguely worded loophole was law, the CIA ran through it as a way of life.

Dulles was considered a genial presence at Georgetown's parties, "with twinkling eyes, a belly laugh, and an almost impish deviousness,"

For a spy, Allen Dulles was a very visible presence in Washington's nightlife when he lived here at 2723 Q Street.

Tim Weiner writes. Gregg Herken writes, "One CIA operative joked to another that if he ever wanted to know what Dulles was up to, all he had to do was read the gossip column in the *Post*." But in his day job, Dulles was ruthless. As a Republican, he had to wait until Eisenhower replaced Truman as president in 1953 before he could lead the agency he'd helped to create, but once there, he wasted no time.

In the 1950s the CIA overthrew governments in Iran and Guatemala; installed governments across the Middle East and in Laos that were supposed to be pro-Western and occasionally were; and trained émigrés and expatriates to undermine governments in Poland, Albania, China, and more—their effort to overthrow the government of Indonesia from 1956 to 1958 was a well-guarded secret and an expensive failure. They plotted assassinations of China's Chou En-lai, the Congo's Patrice Lumumba, the Dominican Republic's Rafael Trujillo, and Cuba's Fidel Castro. They also carried out an extensive program of opening Americans' mail going in and out of the country, and experiments such as Project Artichoke, which gave sometimes-massive, sometimes-marathon doses of LSD to involuntary prisoners

for testing as a truth serum. For Allen Dulles, the son of a preacher, whose grandfather and uncle as well as his brother had served as secretary of state, it was all where the rubber met the road—the sordid means by which the lofty ends of containing and stopping communism would be achieved.

Dulles's CIA made enemies at home as well: Former defense secretary Robert Lovett and well-traveled ambassador David Bruce (the latter a former OSS man and thus no stranger to spying) warned Eisenhower of an out-of-control CIA, but Dulles and the agency continued to work as they wanted, including breaking into Senator Joe McCarthy's office and planting disinformation so as to discredit him.

The obsession with getting Castro, whose Cuba lay just ninety miles off the coast of Florida, was ultimately Dulles's undoing. The disastrous Bay of Pigs operation, in 1961, saw some 1,500 paramilitary troops—armed, trained, and funded by the CIA—land in Cuba with the intention of overthrowing the Castro government. The attempt failed in three days, and the invaders were killed or taken prisoner. Dean Acheson later cracked that it didn't take "Price Waterhouse to discover that 1,500 Cubans weren't as good as 25,000 Cubans," but Dulles later explained that the CIA was under the impression that once the invasion had been launched, President Kennedy would order a full-scale US military invasion if necessary. It didn't work out that way. Dulles was given the National Security Medal on November 28, 1961. He resigned on November 29.

10

DEAN ACHESON

2805 P STREET

ean Acheson was only secretary of state for four years—President Truman's single full term, 1949 to 1953—but in terms of the Cold War, he wasn't exaggerating when he titled his memoir *Present at the Creation*.

Acheson was in on the ground floor of the Truman Doctrine, in which the United States declared that it would stop the spread of communism, as well as the Marshall Plan, the massive economic aid package to Europe without which the Truman Doctrine would likely have failed. He was also in charge of the State Department when the Soviets developed the atomic bomb, when China went from an American ally to a communist country and the United States' proxy enemy in Korea, and when Senator Joseph McCarthy was determined to expunge from the US government anyone he deemed insufficiently loyal by his unclear and shifting standards. The difference between how the world stood before Dean Acheson began to shape it and after is so immense as to dwarf any efforts to explain it.

Born in 1893, Acheson was the son of an Episcopal bishop and went to Yale and Harvard Law. He and his wife, Alice, bought this house without ever having looked inside. He had a dignified, even stuffy, bearing—*New York Times* reporter James "Scotty" Reston said simply, "Dean was not the sort of man you'd hand your hat to by mistake"—but Gregg Herken writes that he was voted "wittiest" and "sportiest" at Yale, where he was a classmate of Averell Harriman and competed on the rowing team; he was fond of saying, "All that I know I learned at my mother's knee and other low joints."

Acheson clerked for Supreme Court Justice Louis Brandeis for two years, then worked in a DC law firm before President Franklin

Dean Acheson had a front-row seat for every major decision that shaped the post–World War II world while he lived at 2805 P Street.

Delano Roosevelt appointed him undersecretary of the treasury. He didn't last long, and returned to private practice before joining the State Department in 1941, overseeing the Lend-Lease Act, under which the United States provided military aid to Great Britain despite not having yet entered the war. He also attended the Bretton Woods Conference of 1944, at which much of the postwar economic world was structured, including the International Monetary Fund, the World Bank, and the forerunner of the World Trade Organization.

In 1945 President Truman appointed Acheson undersecretary of state. Walter Isaacson and Evan Thomas wrote of the Truman-Acheson partnership, "They were one of history's odd couples." Truman was famously a haberdasher from Missouri; Acheson, Ivy League through and through. "Yet they shared a sense of history, irreverence, moral courage, and impatience with waffling."

It seems impossible to believe there was ever a time when opposing the expansion of the Soviet Union was considered by a large faction of the US government to be none of our business, but in the early months of 1947, the nation still had no appetite for such opposition—and Congress, which had just passed into Republican control, was talking more about cutting taxes than providing aid for faraway countries. But Greece and Turkey were teetering on economic ruin, and Great Britain's envoys to the United States had already explained to the American government that they didn't have the money to continue to finance these outposts of their empire. It was more than likely, if someone didn't step in, that the Soviet Union would, and gain itself another two satellite nations pushing west from their borders toward the rest of Europe.

That's when Acheson told Congress that the US and USSR faced off across "an unbridgeable ideological chasm," and, in a precursor to what would soon be called "the domino effect," he warned that without US aid, a communist takeover of Greece and Turkey would lead to the countries of much of the Middle East, as well as perhaps Italy and France, falling to Moscow "like apples in a barrel infected one by one."

Soon after, Acheson lifted a line from a State Department report saying that "it is the policy of the United States to give support to free peoples who are attempting to resist subjugation from armed minorities or from outside forces" and put it into President Truman's

speech to the nation on the subject of economic aid. With one speech and one editing choice, Dean Acheson had largely created what would go on to be known as the Marshall Plan and the Truman Doctrine, respectively, and set the United States on the path of succeeding Great Britain as the dominant power in the world.

The Soviet Union exploded an atomic bomb in 1947; Mao Tsetung's communists came to dominate China in 1949. America's time as the sole superpower was very brief, and many in Congress were looking for an American to blame. Acheson was labeled the "red dean of the cowardly college of containment," a reference to the doctrine that Soviet expert George Kennan drafted and the Truman administration adopted, and when the Korean War broke out, insufficient saber-rattling in a January 1950 Acheson speech was blamed for North Korea's aggression.

Soon, Acheson and his predecessor, George Marshall, were under attack for bumbling in the face of communist ambition. Worse, they and some of Acheson's deputies were in the sights of the Red-hunting Senator Joe McCarthy, who claimed that the State Department "lost China" not through incompetence or, as Acheson described it in a 1950 paper, historical inevitability, but through sympathy for the communist cause. McCarthy could find no other explanation for why a country that had just won World War II seemed to be beset by enemies worldwide: "How can we account for our present situation unless we believe that men high in this government are concerting to deliver us to disaster? This must be the product of a great conspiracy on a scale so immense as to dwarf any previous venture in the history of man." When Acheson refused to turn his back on Alger Hiss, a State Department official convicted of perjury in connection with allegations of communist sympathies, the attacks only continued.

Still, Acheson continued in his post, seeing the United States through the early years of the Cold War when the containment strategy we take for granted was by no means a fait accompli (the possibility of all-out nuclear war with the USSR was discussed on several occasions, and not everyone immediately dismissed the idea). Acheson retired when Truman left office.

He remained an informal adviser to presidents for the rest of his life, including during the Cuban Missile Crisis in 1962, and always showed flashes of wit: A Democrat himself, he considered 1960 pres-

idential candidates Nixon and Kennedy mere "school kids, bright sophomores, and couldn't see how anything either of them had said or done qualified them for the presidency," and described President Johnson as "a real centaur—part man, part horse's ass."

Dean Acheson died in 1971 at his farm in Maryland. Journalist Stewart Alsop later pinpointed it as the date the Establishment died in America. The world had not only changed around Acheson—he'd done more than only a handful of people to change it.

ROBERT JOYCE
2811 O STREET

uring World War II, Robert Joyce left the Foreign Service and joined up with Bill Donovan's Office of Strategic Services (OSS), where his distinctions included trying to recruit Ernest Hemingway to spy on the Nazis. He eventually deemed the writer not reliable enough for that kind of work—the Soviets, who also wanted Hemingway to spy on the Germans, reached the same conclusion.

After the war, Joyce joined George Kennan's Policy Planning Staff (PPS) at the State Department and acted as liaison to the Office of Policy Coordination (OPC), thus becoming one of the players on what Frank Wisner would call his "mighty Wurlitzer"—a multilevel combination of secret plots and dirty tricks ranging from the dead serious (a plot to kill Stalin) to the ludicrous (supplying the Vienna–Budapest train with toilet paper bearing the face of Hungary's top communist). Indeed, while never a part of the OPC or its successor, the CIA, Joyce was once described by one of Wisner's staff as "more CIA than the CIA."

Joyce was one of the leading advocates of "ethnic agent" teams—the training, equipping, and support of paramilitaries among the expatriates of a country that had fallen under communist rule in the hopes they would begin and carry out an overthrow. This was one of the more morally difficult and least effective ideas that the OPC, and later the CIA, threw their muscle behind, and the first—Project Fiend, an attempt beginning in 1949 to restore King Zog to the throne of Albania—was an unmitigated disaster.

"The time is now ripe for us to place greater emphasis on the offensive to consider whether we cannot do more to cause the elimination or at least a reduction of predominant Soviet influence in the

By day, Robert Joyce planned the overthrow of governments; by night, he and his wife were energetic and genial hosts at their 2811 O Street home.

satellite states of Eastern Europe," read a PPS paper Joyce cowrote, and to that end "pixies" began landing on the coast of Albania in October 1949. Enver Hoxha's communist troops were waiting for them—some of them reputedly calling to their would-be invaders by name while moving in on them. In a matter of months, all the "pixies" were captured or killed, or had fled to Greece.

Joyce pressed on, telling his PPS and OPC colleagues that their mission was to "take dynamic steps to reduce the power and influence of the Kremlin inside the Soviet Union and other areas under its control." Indeed, Wisner's OPC, with Joyce's support, was readying similar teams for other Soviet-bloc countries. By 1953, however, the idea had finally run its course. Joyce, before taking a job at the US Embassy in Paris, wrote sagely if cumbersomely, "It is being realized that an intelligence bull is misplaced in the world china shop of 1953 and that a cat and later a soft-treading leopard is a more suitable and effective animal."

But just because you're sending expatriates back to their home countries to face almost-certain death or imprisonment doesn't

mean you can't throw a soiree at night, and the Joyces' house was one of the dinner-party hot spots of Georgetown.

The Joyces were one of the first hosts of the Sunday Night Supper, a social tradition that was born out of necessity (it was traditionally the servants' night off) but became another of the salons at which much of the real work of Washington got done. The Bohlens and Wisners completed the trio of original host couples. Each time, the hosts provided the main dish while guests brought sides, salads, and desserts. In his biography of the Alsop brothers, Robert Merry wrote that the dinners represented a break from the days of DC's "cave dwellers"—families who, it is said, were of such lofty status that they wouldn't usually be able to tell you whether Congress was in session. "In its place was a social hierarchy more closely tied to actual accomplishment and proximity to power. Washington was a world capital now, and the quaint conceits of the old elite didn't carry much weight anymore. The new elite encompassed people with the intelligence and passion to lead America to its postwar destiny."

Robert Joyce spent a year as acting director of the State Department's Bureau of Intelligence and Research before heading to the US consulate in Genoa, Italy. The couple was missed: Joe Alsop wrote to Jane Joyce in the early 1960s, "Washington without the Joyces and with the Wisners about to leave reminds me of the Sahara in the penultimate stage of desiccation when the cattle-keeping people who painted those marvelous pictures the French found were dying off 'round drying water holes."

George Kennan, who, for a short time, lived at 2709 Dumbarton Street, was a principal architect of the Cold War world.

Kennan thought of the Russians as fundamentally a good people, but with an insecurity in foreign relations born of what he described in the telegram (hence the sometimes-stilted syntax) as the nation's beginnings as "a peaceful agricultural people trying to live on vast exposed plain in neighborhood of fierce nomadic peoples."

He continued, "Experience has shown that peaceful and mutually profitable coexistence of capitalist and socialist states is entirely possible," giving World War II as an example. He added that "intervention against USSR . . . is sheerest nonsense. . . . If not provoked by forces of intolerance and subversion, 'capitalist' world of today is quite capable of living at peace with itself and with Russia."

The part everyone remembered came in a sentence from the X article: "It is clear that the main element of any United States policy toward the Soviet Union must be that of a long-term, patient but firm and vigilant containment of Russian expansive tendencies." Within a few years, the concept of containment was the backbone of American policy toward the Soviet Union for the remainder of the latter nation's existence.

Kennan would later say that his policy shouldn't have been construed as a reason for a military buildup: "I should have explained that I didn't suspect them of any desire to launch an attack on us. . . . I didn't think I needed to explain that, but I obviously should have done it." (It wasn't the first or last time he complained that his ideas were sullied by those who implemented them: While he proposed and found the funding for the Office of Policy Coordination, an independent office that conducted covert operations and later merged with the CIA, he said later that he envisioned it as a force that would lie dormant until needed, rather than a permanent organization pulling off dirty tricks around the world.) He felt that the United States and the West could effectively contain communism largely through the example they set of how well people could live in a free society. He also emphasized in the telegram that, while allowing that the struggle would be worldwide, it shouldn't be assumed that all socialist governments or movements would be taking orders directly from the Kremlin—another piece of advice that was largely ignored.

The policy of containment caught on, however, and soon Kennan was in charge of the Policy Planning Staff, the State Department's

main think tank. He didn't last long—actually, he never lasted anywhere for very long.

Averell Harriman once described Kennan as "a man who understood Russia but not the United States." "Almost everyone got annoyed with Kennan after they first got to know him," Kennan's Moscow-embassy colleague Loy Henderson said. "He was so engrossed in his own ideas that he never learned how to go along or get along." Kennan wrote constantly, often many pages of florid prose—not the best prescription for getting your policy papers read. And it wore on him—it's a fool's errand to try to count how many times he threatened to resign whatever job he had.

Partly, it seemed, the stakes he was playing with burdened him. In 1949 he wrote, "We have won great wars and assumed to ourselves great powers. And we have thus become the least free of all peoples. We have placed upon ourselves the obligation to have the answers."

George Kennan finally left the State Department in 1950, returning to Princeton as a lecturer and scholar. He returned to diplomatic service as ambassador to the Soviet Union in 1952 (ironically for such an expert on the country, he only lasted a few months, having done himself in by comparing Stalin to Hitler) and Yugoslavia from 1961 to 1963. Otherwise, he stayed at Princeton for the rest of his life. He died in 2005 at 101.

Late in life, he wrote against the nuclear arms race that a misinterpretation (in his opinion) of his words had caused: "For the love of God, for the love of your children and of the civilization to which you belong, cease this madness. You are mortal men. You are capable of error."

13

JOE ALSOP

2720 DUMBARTON STREET

*T*he same way "Georgetown" became a shorthand term for the new postwar elite in Washington, the high concentration of journalists (along with other high rollers) along this street made the term "Dumbarton Avenue Skeptics" a term for the writers and analysts who put themselves at the center of policy debates in the 1960s and 1970s.

Of all the luminaries in this book, Joe Alsop, who with his brother Stewart wrote the syndicated newspaper column Matter of Fact, may be the one with the widest discrepancy between the power and influence of his heyday and his obscurity now.

Everyone came to this house. When, in 1950, Assistant Secretary of State Dean Rusk needed to be told about the "rather serious border incident" eventually known as the Korean War, they found him here. Late on the first night of his presidency, John F. Kennedy, tired of the inaugural-ball circuit but still pumped full of adrenaline, came here. Hours after Kennedy was told about the Soviet missile bases that spurred the Cuban Missile Crisis, he was at a party here, asking administration members who were guests for advice.

A distant cousin of Eleanor Roosevelt and an unapologetic blueblood from Connecticut, Joe Alsop had been a popular and influential journalist in Washington before World War II. Matter of Fact began December 31, 1945. By November 1946 it was in 57 newspapers, including the *Washington Post*; by the early 1960s, that number was up to 190. The Alsops were also regular contributors to the *Saturday Evening Post*, whose circulation topped out at about six million. At their height, they were as plugged in as it got: "Anything that's known to 15 or 20 people is certainly going to be known to the

Joe Alsop was one of the unofficial rulers of the Georgetown scene, and his house at 2720 Dumbarton Street stands out as much as he did.

Alsop brothers," CIA director Allen Dulles once said. In 1964, President Johnson complained to Defense Secretary McNamara, "I have to rely on Alsop to give [information] to me!"

The *New York Times*'s Arthur Krock told Joe that journalists weren't supposed to be on the dinner-party circuit, but Joe threw twenty-one parties in the first four months of 1946 alone (at the time, he lived at 2709 Dumbarton). Guests included Supreme Court justices, senators, congressmen, journalists, and bureaucrats in the domestic and foreign services. His parties were legendary for vitriolic arguments—"Joe told friends that it was not really considered an argument in the Alsop family until someone had left the table and stormed out of the dining room at least twice," Gregg Herken writes—and the high-level world events at play.

While no utterances from these parties were used verbatim in the column, many of which the Alsops wrote from an office here, all opinions and observations were generally on the record, including those Joe could goad his guests into. Herken describes "the Alsop method" as "bold assertions made on the basis of little or no knowledge, yet in hope that a denial or a contradiction would elicit real information."

The column mixed the Alsops' opinions with solid reporting. They were the first to break the news of George Kennan's "Long Telegram" and the hydrogen bomb. Each brother spoke with at least three government officials a day, face-to-face. They also took marathon trips abroad, reporting on the ground throughout Europe and elsewhere (Joe's reporting from Korea during the war there won multiple awards).

The Alsop brothers' agenda was never far from the surface. Their first column described President Truman as "an average man in a neat gray suit" who wasn't up to the task of the global fight against communism. Joe began issuing warnings about "the new Soviet imperialism" right after World War II; when accused of believing in the "domino effect," he remarked, "Dear boy, I invented it." He and Phil Graham were instrumental in Kennedy's pick of Lyndon B. Johnson for vice president, and never noted when the "missile gap" that helped propel JFK to office mysteriously closed with no explanation.

Joe Alsop was a scrupulous battler, though. He excoriated Truman's secretary of defense, Louis Johnson, blaming his budget-cutting

for creating the atmosphere for the Korean War (more than twenty years later, Joe cited Johnson's resignation as his "most pleasing moment"), and criticized atomic scientist Robert Oppenheimer for his opposition to the hydrogen bomb. Yet the brothers were two of the most prominent journalists to take on Senator Joe McCarthy's witch hunt, calling accusations of conscious disloyalty on the part of their targets ludicrous.

What almost undid Joe was that he was gay. More than once, photos of a 1957 tryst in the USSR threatened to ruin him. He married the former Susan Mary Jay, widow of his Harvard classmate Bill Patten, in 1961 in an attempt to hide his secret; perhaps not surprisingly, they divorced in 1973.

But what did undo Joe was two stories in which his instincts and access led him astray. His anticommunist impulse, and his unwillingness to see that he was being misled by self-dealing sources, prevented him from seeing that Vietnam was different from Korea and World War II; the more vicious and mocking his criticism of his critics became, the harder he fell. And his Nixon administration contacts convinced him Watergate was a minor non-scandal; he later gracefully recognized that the *Post*'s Woodward and Bernstein had beaten him at his own shoe-leather-reporting game.

Joe Alsop retired in 1974 and wrote to the *Times*'s James Reston, "I hope never to talk about politics again." He sold this house that year, moving into 2806 N Street. He died in 1989.

The house, which Joe jokingly described as Garage Palladian, scandalized neighbors. The jarring ochre color and modern design left some neighbors at a loss; others took to Congress, which ran DC even more directly than it does now, and lobbied successfully for a law banning cinder-block houses in Georgetown.

By the way, the question of whether to call it Dumbarton Avenue or Dumbarton Street goes back decades. Suffice it to say, it was originally *Avenue*, and the changeover to *Street* was a very long, haphazard process. Even vintage phone directories go back and forth, and you'll find some groups and institutions still using *Avenue* in their names today.

14

CHIP BOHLEN

2811 DUMBARTON STREET

On October 16, 1962, President Kennedy was at a party at Joe and Susan Mary Alsop's house, but his mind was heavy: Just hours before, he had been informed that the Soviets had nuclear missile bases in Cuba, just ninety miles away from the United States. He was at the party in order to keep up appearances; too many changes to the routine and people, particularly well-connected journalists such as Joe and Stewart Alsop, would have known something was up. It seemed as though the nuclear showdown that everyone in the civilized world had hoped to avoid was coming to pass. Many options were on the table; World War III was one of them.

Kennedy needed advice. He needed to know what the Soviets were thinking, and how they would react in various scenarios. He took one of the guests aside, and they strolled down the path to the Alsops' back garden. In the same manner in which one party guest would ask another about the state of a mutual friend's health, or the availability of a particularly desirable member of the opposite sex, Kennedy asked, "What have the Soviets done historically when their backs are to the wall?" That guest was "Chip" Bohlen.

Charles Bohlen served as ambassador to the Philippines (1957–59) and France (1962-68)—the party at the Alsops' was his going-away party before leaving for Paris—but his real area of expertise was the Soviet Union. Along with George Kennan, he was part of the first American diplomatic mission to the USSR after the United States recognized the Soviet Union in 1933. He was ambassador to the USSR from 1953 to 1957 (succeeding Kennan), and along with Llewellyn "Tommy" Thompson, he was one of Kennedy's "great demonologists"—an expert on the Soviets and their ways.

Chip Bohlen was relied on for his knowledge of the Soviets during disputes between the United States and the Soviet Union. He lived at 2811 Dumbarton Street.

But Bohlen was a diplomat to the core and from the beginning: He joined the Foreign Service straight out of Harvard, and being rather noticeably drunk at the oral examination—despite Prohibition being in effect at the time—proved to be no real impediment. (Indeed, as Evan Thomas and Walter Isaacson wrote, his proclivity for drink was no doubt valuable in his dealings with the Soviets.) His ability to gracefully deal with people from all over the world and from competing bureaucracies made him a perfect foil to the brilliant yet difficult Kennan. Loy Henderson, who also worked at the embassy, said Bohlen "had a pleasing personality, a keen sense of humor, a gift for amusing conversation, and a certain amount of spontaneous joyousness."

Fluent in Russian, Bohlen attended the 1943 Tehran and 1944 Yalta conferences as a translator and assistant to President Roosevelt, and went on several diplomatic missions to the Soviet Union. Later, Senator Joe McCarthy, enraged that the postwar store had supposedly been given away to the Soviets at these conferences, put Bohlen in his sights during Bohlen's hearings to be confirmed as ambassador in 1953; after much talk on both sides, Bohlen was confirmed 74–13. It was a victory for the smooth diplomat and one of McCarthy's first major defeats.

Bohlen was one of the authors of the Marshall Plan and an impetus for Kennan's "Long Telegram," which set forth the principle of containment—the tough but realistic notion that the Soviets could not be defeated but neither should they be ignored and allowed to expand.

Early in his career, Bohlen said, "I know of no one in Russia, whatever his attitude toward the regime, who has felt anything but affection for the Russian people as a whole." Nonetheless, when it came to dealing with Soviet leaders, Bohlen was fond of quoting what he called Lenin's dictum of the bayonet: "Probe with the bayonet. If you meet steel, stop. If you meet mush, push." This served him well during the 1961 Berlin crisis—he told President Kennedy that Khrushchev wouldn't make good on his threat to drive the Western powers out of Berlin, and that the Soviet leader was merely testing his younger counterpart. He was proved right. (Despite Kennedy's having made a beeline to him at the Alsop party regarding the Cuban Missile Crisis, Bohlen played little role in the discussions of the following weeks—a

delay in his deployment, the thinking went, would have tipped off journalists.)

At least one time, however, Bohlen's diplomatic skills failed him: His wife, Avis, was a member of the Cooking Class—a group of Georgetown wives who spent Monday afternoons learning new recipes at the home of former OSS clerk Julia Child (who went on to be TV's first celebrity chef) and then invited their husbands over to enjoy the results. He was booted from the company one night, forced to finish his dinner in the parlor, for lighting up a cigarette at the table. (He fared better than Frank Wisner, who got kicked out entirely for violating Rule One: No criticism of the food.)

Bohlen retired in 1969. It was a short retirement; he had pancreatic cancer. Kennan, with whom he spent decades shaping the postwar world, went to visit him in late 1973 and later said, "We avoided talking about politics, and we really had nothing to say." Chip Bohlen died on January 1, 1974; he was sixty-nine.

15

DREW PEARSON

2820 DUMBARTON STREET

S.O.B.

That was how President Truman described Drew Pearson. He wasn't the only president to have choice words for the columnist—FDR called him a "chronic liar," and JFK once said, "Here I am, president of the United States, and there's nothing I can do to stop Drew Pearson." But S.O.B. is the one that stuck. So many people used it over the decades that Pearson eventually wrote a series of articles titled "Confessions of an S.O.B.," announced that he would title his (never-finished) autobiography *Memoirs of an S.O.B.*, and claimed he wanted his tombstone to read Here Lies an S.O.B. (in the end, that didn't happen). Legend has it that a letter addressed solely to "That S.O.B."—no street address, no city, no state—was delivered to this house.

Pearson's Washington Merry-Go-Round column ran from 1932 to 1969; atypically, it grew out of a pair of books under the same title (written anonymously with Robert S. Allen) rather than the other way around. At its height, the column appeared in more than six hundred American newspapers with a combined circulation of fifty million readers. He also wrote a newsletter and appeared regularly on radio and television.

Drew Pearson was born in Illinois to Quaker parents, and began his writing career with a series of travel articles in 1923. In 1929 he became the Washington correspondent for the *Baltimore Sun*, but was fired when the authorship of the books *Washington Merry-Go-Round* and *More Washington Merry-Go-Round* were made public. He and coauthor Allen were hired to write the column for the *Washington Times-Herald* in 1932; Allen gave up his share of the column after World War II.

Judging by the size of his house at 2820 Dumbarton Street, Drew Pearson's S.O.B. ways were well-rewarded.

Pearson trafficked as much in gossip as in news; he not only had a team of investigators (including Jack Anderson, who went on to become a legendary Washington columnist himself), but was fed information from sources all over Washington who wanted their axes ground in public. And when he needed it, he wasn't above hiring people to break into offices to gain information.

He swung wildly, hard, and often, which means he often really connected: Pearson was perhaps the first journalist, in 1950, to suggest Senator Joe McCarthy wasn't all he was cracked up to be, pointing out some shady entries on his tax returns. McCarthy replied by calling one of Pearson's employees his "KGB handler"—an exaggeration, but the employee was proven decades later to be a KGB source. The senator and the columnist got into a brawl at a private club near Dupont Circle later that year, broken up by none other than Richard Nixon. Pearson also in 1968 reported that "President Johnson is sitting on a political H-bomb—an unconfirmed report that Senator Robert Kennedy may have approved an assassination plot [against Cuban leader Fidel Castro] which then backfired against his late brother." (The "backfiring" part has not been confirmed; the plot was, though not until the release of the CIA's Family Jewels.)

Pearson broke the story of General George Patton slapping a wounded soldier in Sicily, though he wasn't actually there—he ran with

secondhand information that happened to check out. He also said that before World War II, future Secretary of State John Foster Dulles was an agent in providing financial help to the Hitler regime (kind of true). He accused President Kennedy of not having actually written *Profiles in Courage*, which in fact was largely though not totally the work of the future president's chief speechwriter, Ted Sorensen.

But Pearson also went with a story of James Forrestal running away from his wife while she was being mugged in New York in 1937—a story which turned out not to be close to true, which Pearson reportedly knew not to be true, and which may have contributed to the feelings of hopelessness and depression that ultimately led the first secretary of defense to take his own life. He also claimed to have knowledge of a "homosexual ring" running in the office of then–California governor Ronald Reagan. Still, Pearson was reportedly sued for libel 275 times for a total of $200 million and only lost once—a 1953 case against a lawyer whom Pearson had falsely accused of acting as a propagandist for the Dutch government.

Pearson wasn't very welcome at the Georgetown parties, even though he lived in the heart of the neighborhood. While the Alsops, for example, knew how to use information they got at these get-togethers to gather more intelligence in on-the-record interviews the next morning, Pearson couldn't be trusted to play by the acknowledged rules: "'Off the record' meant nothing to him," said Sally Reston, the wife of *New York Times* Washington reporter Scotty Reston—Pearson would use what he heard and overheard directly in his column.

He worked himself hard, what with his various print columns and newsletters, as well as forays into broadcasting. He was successful, as the size and location of this house will attest, but the workload had a cost.

Pearson suffered a heart attack in August 1969. He was told by his doctor to give up all potentially stressful activities—the column, the newsletters, the radio work, even visits to his farm in Potomac, Maryland. Pearson followed orders for about two days. He suffered another episode at the farm on September 1 and died at Georgetown Hospital later that day.

16

FELIX FRANKFURTER

3018 DUMBARTON STREET

orn in Vienna in 1882, Felix Frankfurter was a bit older than most of the rest of the Georgetown Set, but before and during his tenure on the Supreme Court, he was a close adviser to many of them—"a behind-the-scenes manipulator," one history has it, who didn't think his lofty position precluded him from getting into protracted and hidden political discussions.

As a professor at Harvard Law School, one of Frankfurter's students was Dean Acheson, whose Washington career he got started with a letter of recommendation to Supreme Court justice Louis Brandeis. Acheson returned the favor by guiding Frankfurter through the confirmation hearings for his Supreme Court nomination in 1939—the first time a nominee appeared in person before the Senate Judiciary Committee to answer questions. (Acheson advised him, when the question came up, to simply say he was not and had never been a communist, rather than sticking to his original answer, that the question was irrelevant.) Phil Graham, later the publisher of the *Washington Post*, was clerk for Frankfurter, and the justice was valuable in mentoring a young Joe Alsop, who on at least one occasion showed Frankfurter a column before it was published.

As a justice, Frankfurter was part of the conservative bloc of justices: He once wrote that judges "are not legislators, that direct policy-making is not our province," and called Chief Justice Earl Warren's work and thinking "dishonest nonsense." Yet he didn't fit neatly into the classifications we would now call liberal and conservative: A founding member of the American Civil Liberties Union, Frankfurter also sided with the majority in *Korematsu v. United States*, the case that gave the green light to the internment of Japanese-American

Supreme Court Justice Felix Frankfurter was instrumental in bringing the Georgetown Set together from his home at 3018 Dumbarton Street.

citizens during World War II, and *Minersville School District v. Gobitis*, in which the Court ruled that students in public schools could be compelled to salute the flag (the refusal of many Jehovah's Witnesses to do so reportedly resulted in violent reprisals against some of them). He also ruled in the majority in the landmark case *Brown v. Topeka Board of Education*, the 1955 case that ruled school segregation unconstitutional.

Felix Frankfurter suffered a stroke in 1962 and resigned from the Supreme Court; he died in 1965.

Georgetown is a neighborhood like no other, but it's still a neighborhood. Acheson and Frankfurter, the student and the teacher, the secretary of state and the Supreme Court justice, routinely met for breakfast, then walked the streets of the neighborhood to work downtown together. "You couldn't miss them because Acheson towered over Frankfurter," socialite Mimi Crocker once said. "They looked like Mutt and Jeff, each carrying a bulky briefcase and the morning newspaper." One can only imagine the conversations.

17

ALGER HISS

1245 30TH STREET

*T*he accusations surrounding Alger Hiss and his alleged communist leanings were a shot across the bow of the Georgetown establishment—when you see how settled into the area Hiss's house was (he had had other residences a bit farther out from the center of Georgetown), it's easy to perceive the Hiss affair as an attack not only on one man, but the entire neighborhood. And though the charges were never conclusively proven, the ripple effects lasted years, even decades.

Hiss was born in Baltimore in 1904, graduated from Harvard Law School, and went into government service in 1933, shifting over to the State Department three years later. During World War II his distinctions included acting as executive secretary of the Dumbarton Oaks Conference, at which the basic plans for the United Nations were laid, and attending the 1945 Yalta Conference, at which Roosevelt, Churchill, and Stalin met to discuss the endgame in Europe once Hitler was defeated. He also served as secretary-general of the UN Charter Conference in San Francisco.

Hiss returned to the private sector in 1946. But in 1948 Whittaker Chambers, a former *Time* magazine editor and admitted communist, told the House Un-American Activities Committee that Hiss had been a member of a communist front group since the 1930s. It wasn't the first rumbling in Hiss's direction—Soviet defectors and Americans caught spying for Moscow said that Hiss was indeed a communist, though a thoroughly American one. A couple days later, Hiss testified to the committee that he had never been a communist and no idea who Chambers was. Hiss eventually said that he had sublet an apartment to Chambers after Hiss and his wife, Priscilla, moved into this house, but that Chambers had used a different name.

Alger Hiss lived here at 1245 30th Street while he responded to accusations of being a communist.

When Chambers repeated his allegations against Hiss on *Meet the Press* (at the time a radio show), Hiss sued him for defamation. Chambers responded by claiming he would prove that Hiss was not only a homegrown communist, but a spy. He produced evidence of State Department documents that Priscilla had retyped, as well as photos of documents—some classified, some not—that he said Hiss had given him back in 1938. Chambers had hidden the photos in a hollowed-out pumpkin on his farm in Salisbury, Maryland, the previous day. The cache of evidence came to be known as the Pumpkin Papers.

While the statute of limitations had run out on the accusations against Hiss, he was charged with perjury for allegedly lying to Congress about never having met Chambers. His first trial resulted in a hung jury, with Chambers admitting he'd lied in some previous testimony, but on retrial Hiss was convicted. In January 1950 he was sentenced to five years in prison. He ended up serving three.

Response to the verdict in the neighborhood was muted, except for Hiss's former boss, Secretary of State Dean Acheson, who lived just a few blocks away and was a law partner of Hiss's brother Donald. True to his principled yet sometimes haughty form, Acheson said shortly after the sentencing that "I do not intend to turn my back on Alger Hiss." Communist-hunters leapt at the statement—if Acheson wouldn't turn his back on a supposedly proven communist, he was clearly in on whatever large-scale conspiracy to sell out the United States the highest levels of the government were supposedly engaged in. Acheson was bedeviled by accusations of disloyalty against himself and members of his department for the remainder of his tenure.

The question of whether Hiss was wrongly convicted has never gone away. Hiss claimed that the papers supposedly retyped by his wife were forgeries, made from a typewriter rigged up to type exactly like his. It's not quite as outlandish as it sounds—the OSS did such things during World War II. But no definitive proof was found either way. Hiss, who had been disbarred, was eventually readmitted.

When the Soviet Union broke up in 1992, Hiss asked for an examination of their files in an effort to prove his innocence; no evidence of collusion with Moscow was found, but the examination was too cursory to be definitive. In 1995 the existence of a World War II army

counterintelligence program called Venona was acknowledged and thousands of cables released; they fairly conclusively proved that Julius Rosenberg was in fact a Soviet spy and strongly implicated Hiss. Still, other examinations of the Venona evidence claim that the case against Hiss is inconclusive.

One thing is for sure, however: The Hiss verdict was a political and publicity-based bonanza for two conservative politicians.

A few weeks after the sentencing, Senator Joseph McCarthy gave his famous Wheeling, West Virginia, speech in which he held up a sheet of paper and claimed, "I have here in my hand a list" of known communists in the State Department. He almost immediately vaulted from being best known (in one poll's findings) as the worst senator in Washington to virtually running the town with his infamous Senate committee for the next three years.

And a House Un-American Activities Committee member kept the pursuit of Hiss alive when it looked its weakest—right after Hiss's first HUAC testimony, when President Truman pressured the committee to give it up. This member found Hiss "insolent," "condescending," and "insulting in the extreme," and took the lead in calling Acheson's defense of Hiss "disgusting" for its signal of the betrayal of America's highest ideals. He parlayed the exposure from the Hiss affair into election to the Senate in 1950 and the vice presidency in 1952. His name was Richard Nixon.

Neither McCarthy nor Nixon lived in Georgetown.

18

GORDON GRAY
1224 30TH STREET

ordon Gray never held the sexiest jobs in Washington, but he served as a foreign-policy adviser, among other things, to presidents of both parties for nearly thirty years.

Born in Baltimore and a product of the University of North Carolina and Yale Law School, Gray, the son of a tobacco executive, was living in North Carolina at the time of the attack on Pearl Harbor. Despite being thirty-two, a newspaper publisher, a state senator, and married with three children, he not only enlisted in the army, but went in as a private, disdaining the automatic commission he was offered. He rose from private to captain in three years of army service during World War II, then served as assistant secretary of the army in 1947 and secretary in 1950. Each job he took with the understanding that he'd be headed back to North Carolina soon. Yet he couldn't escape. "This public service bug that had bitten me almost always kept me from saying 'no' to something that I thought was perhaps important."

For example, he once said that he never wanted the job as secretary of the army, preferring to take the post of dean of the business school at the University of North Carolina, but took the army post after President Truman resignedly said that he'd have to go back to the Senate and say he'd made a mistaken appointment: "Suddenly it dawned on me you don't do that kind of thing to a President of the United States, you know."

Gray served as president of the University of North Carolina from 1950 to 1955, then served as national security adviser under President Eisenhower from 1958 to 1961. From there he was appointed to the President's Intelligence Advisory Board, where he served until 1977—

A dedicated public servant, Gordon Gray split his time between 1224 30th Street in the District and North Carolina.

from the Kennedy to Ford administrations. He also served on boards to reform and standardize the codes of justice across branches of the military and to reform and reorganize the National Guard, and was director of the Psychological Strategy Board (devoted to such messaging and propaganda as Radio Free Europe), chairman of the Commission on the Financing of Hospital Care, a member of the President's Committee on International Information Activities, and director of the Office of Defense Mobilization. "Gray board," the *New York Times* later said, was a term used in Washington for the kind of vital panels he sat on.

Gray was best known for serving on the Atomic Energy Commission's Personnel Security Board, which reviewed the security clearance of pioneering nuclear scientist J. Robert Oppenheimer after he committed the sin of coming out against the hydrogen bomb. The board found that Oppenheimer was a loyal American, but that renewing his clearance was not in the interest of national security.

Gordon Gray's desire to serve the public interest was balanced by his ability to take or leave any particular job. "I always took the

position, in any public job I had, that I didn't care whether I had it the next day or not, and that was the hallmark, I think, of good public servants," he once said. He died in 1982. His son, C. Boyden Gray, served as White House counsel to President George H. W. Bush and ambassador to the European Union for President George W. Bush.

19

BEN BRADLEE AND SALLY QUINN
3014 N STREET

*I*f an average American can come up with the name of one newspaper editor, it's probably Ben Bradlee's. He set the standard for editors—tough, demanding, yet always willing to go to the wall for his reporters and to mix things up.

Benjamin Crowninshield Bradlee—his family background is as WASPish as his name sounds—was born in Boston in 1921. A bout with polio at age fourteen forced him to abandon sports and take up debating and writing. He went to Harvard, of course—he was said to be the fifty-second male Bradlee to attend Harvard since 1795 and wrote that "no alternatives were suggested, or contemplated"—and worked in naval intelligence during World War II. He began in journalism as a reporter at the *New Hampshire Sunday News*, a newspaper he cofounded; worked at *Newsweek*, eventually rising to become Washington bureau chief; and returned to the *Washington Post* in 1965 (after having been there briefly in the forties) as managing editor, followed by executive editor in 1968.

"I like a nice, rowdy metropolitan newspaper," he once said, and the worst comment he would make on a story was "mego"—short for "my eyes glaze over." Working in partnership with publisher Katharine Graham, Bradlee doubled the size of the newspaper's reporting staff; before long circulation doubled as well. Before he got there, the paper had won four Pulitzer prizes, only one for reporting; in his twenty-three years at the helm, it won seventeen.

Larry Kramer, publisher of *USA Today*, worked for Bradlee at the *Post* and said of his style, "If you worked for him you barely realized you had become unflinchingly loyal to him. His advice was so grounded in just doing the right thing that sometimes you didn't even realize he had given you advice and you were following it."

Ben Bradlee and Sally Quinn threw some memorable bashes for Washington society at their home at 3014 N Street.

Bradlee was a longtime friend of the Kennedy clan, and *Newsweek* was given the scoop when Gary Powers's U-2 spy plane was shot down over the USSR in 1960. He was one of the first to see Jackie Kennedy after her husband's murder. "There is no more haunting sight in all the history I've observed," he later wrote, "than Jackie Kennedy, walking slowly, unsteadily into those hospital rooms, her pink suit stained with her husband's blood."

The *Post* was involved with two momentous stories in the early 1970s: the Pentagon Papers and Watergate. In the former, the Defense Department's "secret history" of the Vietnam War—quite different from the version the public had gotten—became available to the *New York Times*. After a federal court stopped the *Times* from publishing the papers (the first time an American court had ever stopped a newspaper from publishing something, as opposed to penalizing them for it afterward), the *Post* obtained them. Bradlee, Graham, more top editors, and a large number of lawyers argued about what to do with them. Eventually, they went ahead and published stories based on the papers, and the courts upheld their right to do so.

Watergate was the story on which the *Washington Post* and Bradlee made their national reputation: What seemed a low-level break-in at Democratic National Headquarters at the Watergate Hotel became a little more interesting to rookie crime reporters Bob Woodward and Carl Bernstein when they noticed that one of the burglars had worked for Nixon's reelection campaign. It was a slender thread, but they and Bradlee pulled at it for more than two years until the Nixon White House unraveled, and the president resigned amid the exposure of his administration's lawlessness and his personally ordering the obstruction of justice.

Through it all, Graham let it be known throughout Washington that the *Post* would not be intimidated, while Bradlee and others worked directly with Woodward and Bernstein to make sure they had the story and had it straight. Woodward recalled, "He was a doubter, a skeptic—'Do we have it yet?' 'Have we proved it?'" He added that the words he most dreaded to hear from Bradlee were "You don't have it yet, kid."

"Ben . . . set the ground rules—pushing, pushing, pushing, not so subtly asking everyone to take one more step, relentlessly pursuing the story in the face of persistent accusations against us and a concerted campaign of intimidation," Graham wrote in her memoir, *Personal History*.

For Bradlee's part, he said the Pentagon Papers was the bigger of the two stories—"Watergate cast a bigger shadow, but there was no time in Watergate when we had to tear everything apart and make a single decision that was fraught with such consequence"—and of all his efforts, he felt the introduction of the Style section was his biggest innovation, replacing the old "women's pages" with an ongoing section that went beyond a single story into "a way of interpreting society." He was badly burned in 1981, however, when reporter Janet Cooke resigned and returned her Pulitzer Prize when she eventually admitted her story about an eight-year-old heroin addict was made up.

Bradlee and Sally Quinn, his third wife, were staples of the Georgetown party circuit, throwing more than a few bashes themselves. Woodward and Bernstein wrote that Bradlee could "grind his cigarettes out in a demitasse cup during a formal dinner party," yet was "one of the few persons who could pull that kind of thing off and leave the hostess saying how charming he was."

And while the Washington party scene was essentially an unofficial branch of government, Sally Quinn was one of the first to consider it worth documenting. Bradlee hired her at the *Post* in 1973; they married in 1978. She reportedly wrote about the party circuit because no one else wanted to, but she quickly became a chronicler of the on- and off-record dealings that went on over drinks and appetizers, sometimes breaking news that the *Post*'s hard-bitten reporters couldn't get. Once called a "social terrorist," Quinn herself said, "I covered [parties] the way someone in the Metro section covered a crime." Henry Kissinger, used to dealing with presidents, generals, and dictators, once said, "I was always afraid of Sally Quinn."

Ben Bradlee died in 2014. He was ninety-two.

Across the street at number 3017, set far back and protected by pillars and large trees, stands the house that Jacqueline Kennedy and her two children lived in for nearly a year in 1964 after President Kennedy's assassination, having first stayed a few months in Averell Harriman's house at 3038. Legend has it she went off for a weekend trip to New York City in 1964 and came back marveling that no one had recognized her. She and the children moved there soon after.

ABE FORTAS

3025 N STREET

*A*be Fortas was once Lyndon B. Johnson's personal lawyer, instrumental to Johnson's rise to the US Senate, then later the vice presidency and presidency. He remained a confidant to Johnson and was rewarded with a seat on the US Supreme Court, where he did some landmark work—before resigning in a cloud of scandal and with his name linked to what has been described as one of the biggest blunders in recent presidential history.

Born and raised in Memphis, Fortas was a law professor at Yale and a member of some of the delegations involved with the establishment of the United Nations. In private practice, he represented Johnson in a ballot-challenge case regarding the Texas Democratic senatorial primary, winning Johnson a spot on the ballot, which the future president turned into the Senate seat that became his launching pad.

Before reaching the Supreme Court, Fortas had argued before it in landmark cases including 1963's *Gideon v. Wainwright*, in which the court ruled that the state has an obligation to provide a defendant a lawyer if he or she can't afford one.

One history has it that President Johnson picked Fortas to be his eyes and ears on the high court—to let him know whether any of Johnson's Great Society programs were on the verge of being ruled unconstitutional. It's true that the amount of communication between the president and the justice was unusual, even for old colleagues.

On the Supreme Court, Fortas was a key figure in some landmark cases regarding the juvenile justice system—in one case, he pointed out the unfairness of sentencing a fifteen-year-old to juvenile prison until his twenty-first birthday for a crime for which the maximum

Supreme Court justice Abe Fortas lived here at 3025 N Street. His nomination to the chief justice's seat was called "one of the most consequential blunders in modern American politics."

penalty for an adult was two months in jail or a $50 fine. He wrote majority opinions in cases that established that juveniles had a right to a lawyer and that protected students' expression in school: Neither "students or teachers shed their constitutional rights to freedom of speech or expression at the schoolhouse gate," he wrote.

When Johnson nominated Fortas for chief justice in 1968, the knives were out. Senate conservatives, already unhappy with the liberal record of the court under retiring Chief Justice Earl Warren, grilled Fortas on his relationship with Johnson, and a scandal was brought to light involving an eye-popping set of speaking fees that Fortas collected from American University, the money for which came from a group of companies that might have business before the court. Republicans announced that they would filibuster the nomination, and Fortas asked that he be withdrawn. The slot stayed open until the conservative Warren Burger was nominated by Johnson's successor, Richard Nixon. The chief justice's chair has been in conservative, Republican-appointed hands ever since. In the *New York Times*, David Leonhardt called the Fortas nomination "one of the most consequential blunders in modern American politics."

Another scandal emerged in 1969: Fortas, still an associate justice, had in 1966 signed for a lifetime retainer from Louis Wolfson, a Wall Streeter who was under investigation at the time. With Nixon in the White House, Fortas's champion was gone. He resigned later that year. He returned to private practice, often arguing in front of his former colleagues, including Harry Blackmun, the man appointed to replace him, until he died in 1982. A lifelong violin player, he was part of the semiformal N Street Strictly-no-refunds String Quartet, which played in the neighborhood and often featured distinguished musicians who were in town.

21

AVERELL HARRIMAN

3038 N STREET

mbassador-at-large was only one of the many job titles W. Averell Harriman held in his life, but it's the one that describes him best. For four decades, when there was an important international conversation to be had, Harriman was the man a Democratic president wanted there.

Harriman was the son of a railroad tycoon who was said to have told him, "Great wealth is an obligation." Averell took the point, once saying, "It is as indefensible for a man who has capital not to apply himself to using it in a way that will be of most benefit for the country as it is for a laborer to refuse to work." He advised presidents Roosevelt, Truman, Kennedy, and Johnson. During the Democratic presidential interregnum of Eisenhower's two terms, he ran twice unsuccessfully for the Democratic nomination for president (losing both times to Adlai Stevenson) and successfully for governor of New York; he served from 1955 to 1958.

Harriman first visited the Soviet Union in 1926 on a business trip, and he was ambassador to Moscow during most of World War II, also serving as an adviser to President Roosevelt at the Yalta Conference. He had many arguments, often fierce, with Soviet leader Joseph Stalin, especially toward the end of the war when it seemed as though, once Hitler was out of the way, Soviet-American conflict of one kind or another would be inevitable. But they always respected each other: Stalin once gave Harriman a white stallion that the ambassador had admired in a Soviet military film.

"We must have our hand out in friendship but our guard up," he told President Truman at the end of the war. James Forrestal, who became the first secretary of defense, said Harriman told him "the

"The Crocodile" Averell Harriman brought decades of experience in foreign relations when he lived at 3038 N Street and was called upon to advise presidents.

outward thrust of Communism was not dead and that we may have to face an ideological warfare just as vigorous and dangerous as Fascism or Nazism."

After the war, Harriman was switched over to become ambassador to London, but only served there for a few months before President Truman had a new job for him: secretary of commerce. He chaired a committee tasked with compiling a report on how the proposed Marshall Plan, a multibillion-dollar aid package, would rebuild postwar Western Europe and not incidentally keep those nations' economies healthy enough that the citizenry wouldn't heed the siren call of communism. "More than any other government document, the final report of the Harriman Committee converted the press to the cause of the true believers," one observer wrote.

After the Marshall Plan was approved, Harriman left the Commerce Department post to spend the next few years traveling throughout Europe overseeing the disbursement of the money (some of which was siphoned off to finance the Office of Policy Coordination, the innocent-sounding name for an early version of the CIA).

Evan Thomas and Walter Isaacson write, "There is no equivalent in today's foreign policy bureaucracy to Harriman's position or his power. The immensity and urgency of the task demanded a benevolent despot." They compare the power President Truman gave him to the power FDR and Marshall gave General Eisenhower during the war.

After Kennedy restored the Democratic Party to the White House, Harriman was back in his accustomed role: leading international negotiations, particularly (though not exclusively) with the Soviets. He represented the United States at multinational talks on the future of Laos, talks with the USSR to ban aboveground nuclear weapons, and the early meetings of the Paris conference seeking to end the Vietnam War.

He was nicknamed "The Crocodile" for his ability to seem disinterested and dull, then suddenly snap into a speaker with a question that would bring the entire issue into a new perspective (and often shut said speaker down). During nuclear test-ban talks in 1963, one official said, "He just keeps on talking in that low monotone," and the journalist Theodore White wrote that "people . . . think he is stupid" (White disagreed). In his obituary, the *New York Times* wrote, "His style was not of the outgoing warmth generally associated with the successful politician, but it fitted the successful negotiator perfectly."

Averell Harriman was indefatigable: He was seventy-two when he negotiated that ban on aboveground nuclear tests, seventy-six when he became the first American delegate to the Paris negotiations aimed at ending the Vietnam War, and had informal talks with Soviet premier Yuri Andropov as late as 1983. He died in 1986 at ninety-four. Afterwards, his wife, Pamela, freed from the nonpartisanship she had to maintain as a diplomat's wife, became a major power player in the Democratic Party, most notably giving an invaluable boost to a little-known 1992 presidential candidate named Bill Clinton, who later said he wouldn't have made it to the White House without her support.

Pulitzer Prize–winning historian Arthur Schlesinger was the scribe of the Georgetown Set and made his home here at 3122 O Street.

He was rewarded for his work with a spot in the Kennedy administration. Later asked whether he took Schlesinger on to write the official history of the administration, the president said he would write it himself, but added that "Arthur will probably write his own, and it will be better for us if he's in the White House, seeing what goes on, instead of reading about it in the *New York Times* and *Time* magazine."

Schlesinger's history of the Kennedy presidency, *A Thousand Days*, won him his second Pulitzer Prize, as well as the National Book Award. He was unabashed in his admiration for the ideals and energy of the Kennedy White House: "Meetings were continuous. The evenings too were lively and full. The glow of the White House was lighting up the whole city. . . . Never had girls seemed so pretty, tunes so melodious, an evening so blithe and unconstrained." He later said, "Working for him was the most exhilarating experience."

His obvious enthusiasm for the Kennedy White House, and his overlooking of the president's dalliances with women, were criticized as partisanship masquerading as scholarship. Schlesinger replied that, as far as the extramarital affairs went, it had no effect on Kennedy's ability to do his job, and as for his partisan connections, "Being an historian does not require one to renounce being a citizen. [The British historian Thomas Babington] Macaulay was a member of parliament. You shift gears when you write history; everyone does."

He continued to write landmark histories and work in politics, joining Robert F. Kennedy's campaign in 1968 and Edward Kennedy's in 1980. He eventually wrote more than twenty books, including *The Vital Center*, *The Imperial Presidency*, and *Robert F. Kennedy and His Times*, finishing with *War and the American Presidency* in 2004, in which he called the invasion and occupation of Iraq "a ghastly mess."

"The historical mind can be analytical, or it can be romantic," Schlesinger once wrote. "The best historians are both."

Schlesinger also taught at Harvard, Princeton, and the City University of New York, and was a frequent companion of Jacqueline Kennedy's after her husband's assassination. He died in New York in 2007; he was eighty-nine. "I have lived through interesting times," he once wrote, "and had the luck of knowing some interesting people."

Henry Cabot Lodge lived here at 3132 O Street, not far from his longstanding political adversary, John F. Kennedy.

high US officials, was at least a bystander and at most an active participant in the coup against South Vietnamese leader Ngo Dinh Diem in 1963, which led to the leader's death and instituted the very political instability it was intended to stave off.

If any other evidence was needed to explain how the political campaigns of old differ from modern-day electioneering, Lodge's experience in the 1964 Republican nomination process should suffice: It was only after winning the New Hampshire primary over Barry Goldwater and Nelson Rockefeller that Lodge decided that he should perhaps consider running. (He didn't.)

Henry Cabot Lodge was reappointed ambassador to South Vietnam by President Johnson, then worked as ambassador to West Germany and the Holy See before retiring in 1977. He died in 1985.

Stewart Alsop lived four blocks from Joe Alsop at 3139 Dumbarton Street.

the mid-1950s he was emerging from his brother's shadow: While Joe was on a long reporting trip to the Middle East and France in 1957, Stewart and his wife, Tish, hosted the annual "Alsop ball," with more than a hundred guests including senators, ambassadors, and diplomats. ("Unlimited champagne and unlimited coffee is, I have concluded, the basic formula," he later wrote to Joe.)

While the brothers wrote joint pieces for the *Saturday Evening Post* through the 1950s, Stewart began to pick up new writing partners for such articles, and started to strike out on his own as well. He also began to make appearances on television, which Joe once called the one technology he wished he could un-invent. By 1958 Stewart was ready to dissolve the partnership: Like "a pair of middle aged cart horses, who had been in harness together for a long time," he wrote to Joe, he had begun "to chafe a bit."

Stewart took off on his own, becoming a regular contributor to the *Saturday Evening Post* through 1968, then a columnist for *Newsweek*. While he wasn't without the kind of blind spots that characterized the Alsop style—he cowrote probably the seminal story that cast Kennedy as the clear-eyed hero who faced down the Soviets during the Cuban Missile Crisis with nothing but steely resolve—he never suffered the same kind of loss of reputation that Joe eventually did. He met criticism of the Vietnam War with vehement disagreement, but not the kind of outright ridicule that backfired on his older brother.

Stewart Alsop's career and life were cut short, however—he was diagnosed with leukemia in 1973, wrote "a sort of memoir" about his battle that year, and died in 1974. He was sixty.

"I remember sitting with him on my back terrace the spring before he died," Graham writes, "with him knowing he'd likely never see another Washington springtime, and watching him look wistfully out over the flowers and the blooming trees. It was clearer to me than ever how much he loved this city."

While their breakup had been acrimonious at the time, Joe Alsop titled his memoir *"I've Seen the Best of It"*—reportedly one of Stewart's last utterances.

25

AU PIED DE COCHON (NOW A FIVE GUYS)

1335 WISCONSIN AVENUE

This entry is a little out of our time frame, but it's right on our trail and it's too good to pass up.

In the summer of 1985, KGB agent Vitaly Yurchenko defected to the United States while he was on assignment in Rome. He quickly proved his value by naming two American intelligence agents who were working for the Soviet Union—one of whom was convicted, the other of whom fled the country. It all seemed to be working out pretty well for both sides.

On Saturday, November 2, 1985, Yurchenko and his CIA handler walked into Au Pied de Cochon, a French restaurant that inhabited the building that now houses Five Guys Burgers and Fries, for a meal. Yurchenko excused himself to go to the bathroom. Once there, he hoisted himself out the bathroom window and made haste for the Soviet compound (now the Russian Embassy) farther up Wisconsin Avenue, in the Glover Park neighborhood. A couple days later, he left for the Soviet Union, but not before denouncing the United States and claiming he'd been kidnapped.

There's no shortage of speculation as to why he had such a change of heart. It's said that he had a mistress in Ottawa who he thought would defect herself to join him, and that Soviet authorities, who knew about their affair, wouldn't let her out of their sight after Yurchenko's defection. (A former KGB man says Yurchenko was allowed to go to her door and ask her to come with him, but she declined.) It's also said that Yurchenko was a hypochondriac who was certain he had advanced stomach cancer, and once an American doctor told him he was fine, he realized he'd made a big mistake. It's said that one of his CIA debriefers was Aldrich Ames, who later

The former Au Pied du Cochon, site of Vitaly Yurchenko's Last Supper.

defected to the Soviet Union, and that Ames either said or intimated that Yurchenko would never feel truly safe in the States. It's also said that Yurchenko was a plant, anyway—that the agents he exposed were no big deal, really, and that he received a medal upon his return to the Soviet Union for his successful "infiltration operation." (Of course they would say that, others say.)

Short of heading to Moscow, where Yurchenko still lives, it's impossible to know exactly what happened—and given his track record, you might not get the straight story even then. One thing that's for sure, however, is that to this day a plaque affixed to the booth he left from reads "V. Yurchenko: Last supper in the USA, Saturday, November 2nd, 1985."

Of course, with the Cold War over, who knows? He might come back.

MARTIN'S TAVERN

1264 WISCONSIN AVENUE

*M*artin's Tavern is one of the oldest saloons in Georgetown. Located at the corner of Wisconsin and N Street, it figured prominently in the lives of JFK and Jackie.

From the point that John F. Kennedy frequented Martin's as a freshman senator, he would continue on to serve a term and a half in the US Senate and two-plus years as the president of the United States. He would famously proclaim the United States to be "on the edge of a New Frontier"; explain that a Roman Catholic could serve as president without taking orders from Rome; squeak by Vice President Richard Nixon in the 1960 election; exhort his fellow Americans to "ask not what your country can do for you; ask what you can do for your country"; take the country through the emerging Cold War's first major confrontation during the Cuban Missile Crisis, which saw Soviet nuclear weapons within a hundred miles of the United States; blunder through the Bay of Pigs "invasion" (one could charitably call it) of Cuba by a bumbling group of US-trained expatriates; establish the Peace Corps, which gave invaluable aid to disadvantaged people worldwide and gave Americans a chance to see the world and serve something larger than themselves without fighting in a war; conduct extramarital affairs that were the stuff of legend and an enduring symbol of a very different relationship between presidents and the press; begin the intervention of active US troops in Vietnam, a war that would last in one form or another for nearly twenty years; enthrall an encircled Berlin by telling its citizens "Ich bin ein Berliner"; and be gunned down during a motorcade in Dallas, the first president to be assassinated in more than sixty years and the last one to date.

Martin's Tavern, at 1264 Wisconsin Avenue, hosted the marriage proposal that started Camelot.

Jacqueline Bouvier would go on to have two children, as well as a miscarriage and a son who lived for two days; restore the White House to historic importance; compose one-half of the couple that created a time in American history still referred to as Camelot; charm much of the world with her worldly yet vivacious energy; see her husband gunned down beside her and die in front of her; request and light the eternal flame that burns at his grave in Arlington National Cemetery; captivate the world again with the strength and dignity with which she bore her loss; cause raised eyebrows nationwide when she married the Greek shipping tycoon Aristotle Onassis less than five years later; become a widow again seven years after that; continue working for her passions of historic preservation and relative privacy and safety for her children, whose father and uncle had been assassinated; and pass away in 1994.

But on June 26, 1953, he was thirty-six and a new senator and she was twenty-three, and in the high-powered atmosphere of Martin's, they probably blended in reasonably well with all the other young couples who came (and still come) to the pub every Friday night as they sat in a booth overlooking N Street—a booth marked by a plaque today—and he asked her to marry him. The Parker House Hotel in Boston claims the proposal happened there, but Martin Snoak says he saw it with his own two eyes and told a Washington TV station in 2015 that "I didn't think of it as anything unusual."

She said yes.

27

STUART SYMINGTON
3263 N STREET

*A*s has previously been noted, perhaps nothing separated
the denizens of Georgetown quite like the Vietnam War
did. In the far-off conflict, the idea that the United States
should "stand up" to Soviet "aggression" wherever and however it
presented itself got its mightiest stretch: The assertion that Vietnam was essential to American interests was a hard sell to a lot of
people, and Stuart Symington, one of Joe Alsop's most frequent
dinner guests, was one of them. Notably, however, he didn't start
off his public life as a pursuer of peace—he was the first secretary
of the air force.

Symington was born in Amherst, Massachusetts, in 1901, grew
up in Baltimore, and began a career in business. During World War II
he transformed his company, Emerson Electric, in St. Louis, into the
largest manufacturer of gun turrets for American bombers. After the
war he was rewarded with a spot in government, running the Sur-
plus Property Board—dedicated to selling or otherwise disposing of
the great stores of stuff the United States had built up for the now-
finished war—and eventually worked his way up to assistant secretary of war. When the air force was established as an independent
branch of the military in 1947, he was picked to run it.

The air force's greatest accomplishment during Symington's run
was probably the Berlin Airlift. In 1948 a force of American and British bombers brought food and other supplies to the people of Berlin,
a city that was divided into four quadrants (American, Soviet, British,
and French) but was wholly within the Soviet-controlled part of Germany and was being blockaded over a currency dispute. The massive
operation lasted from July 1948 to April 1949 and cost the modern
equivalent of billions of dollars (between the US, UK, and Germany)

Stuart Symington was one of the first proponents of the Vietnam War—and one of its first high-level opponents. He made his home here at 3263 N Street.

and more than a hundred lives in accidents, but the city survived the blockade and the Soviets eventually backed down.

Still, by 1950 Symington had had enough of the postwar budget reductions that hit all of the American military. After the Soviets had detonated their first nuclear bomb, he continued to protest his funding cuts as a false economy, on several occasions saying, "What the hell good is it to be the richest man in the graveyard?" He resigned that year, though he spent the next two years in other administration posts before winning election to the Senate from Missouri in 1952.

Symington was a prominent voice in the Senate for a stronger national defense, but was also a constant thorn in the side of Senator Joe McCarthy as a minority-party member of McCarthy's Senate Committee on Investigations. His criticisms of the Wisconsin senator's single-minded, ruinous pursuit of communists in the US government earned him the nickname "Sanctimonious Stu" from McCarthy, to whom Symington more than once recommended psychiatric care.

Along with senator and future vice president Lyndon B. Johnson and others, Symington was a loud voice protesting the "missile gap" that Republican President Eisenhower's administration had allowed to grow between the United States and the Soviet Union. Symington ran for the Democratic nomination for president in 1956 and 1960, losing to Adlai Stevenson and John F. Kennedy, respectively. After Kennedy won, it became known that the missile gap was largely illusory. This was perhaps an accident, perhaps not (given the close relationship between missile-gap megaphone Joe Alsop and Kennedy).

But in the late 1960s, when it was becoming clear that US involvement in Vietnam was much different, longer, and less successful than advertised, Symington joined a high-profile group of senators who rescinded their early support of the war. By 1975, when Symington announced his retirement, he said, "I'm tired of having old men in government passing laws that force young men to do battle in causes that are not essential to the United States." He died in 1988.

28

JOHN F. KENNEDY

3307 N STREET

The future president, and later his family, lived in many George-town locations, including just a few blocks away from this house at 3260 N Street before he and Jacqueline Bouvier married, as well as in two houses on P Street and one on Dent Place. But this house was the Kennedy family's last stop before the White House, where the future president, wife Jackie, and their children lived from June 1957 until moving to Pennsylvania Avenue in January 1961.

It was while living here that he won his final Senate election, over Boston lawyer Vincent Celeste, in 1958, giving Kennedy his second Senate term. It was also while living here that Kennedy decided to run for president in 1960, the campaign during which he gave his New Frontier speech, the one that laid out a forthright progressive agenda for the 1960s: He may have promised that "we stand today on the edge of a New Frontier," but in a precursor to the "ask not" passage from his inaugural address, Kennedy said, "But the New Frontier of which I speak is not a set of promises—it is a set of chal-lenges. It sums up not what I intend to offer the American people, but what I intend to ask of them."

Kennedy's term as president was one of the most active in his-tory, in terms of getting bills passed through Congress and enacted. It was also the presidency that ensnared the United States more deeply in Vietnam, brought about the disaster of the Bay of Pigs, and continued the lack of restraint of the CIA—all the dark flipside of the can-do spirit that characterized Kennedy's approach to domestic affairs. All of which was a piece of the ethos of the Georgetown Set.

The story of John F. Kennedy's life, presidency, and legacy has filled many books. The immediate, and visceral, impact of the 1960

John F. Kennedy and his family lived here at 3307 N Street before decamping to the White House.

election was the elevation of one of the Georgetown Set to the highest office in the land—perhaps, the world. Newspapermen such as Joe Alsop, Phil Graham, and Ben Bradlee offered advice and counsel before and during the campaign; Alsop, who was instrumental in Kennedy's pick of Lyndon B. Johnson as vice president, was particularly said to be over the moon when the election results came in. It's hard to know how much of the liberal-yet-hawkish agenda of the Kennedy and Johnson years would have been instituted under a President Nixon elected in 1960—certainly some, certainly not all.

Two events give testimony to what a neighborhood, as well as nationwide, commotion Kennedy's election and assassination must have caused:

On the east-facing wall of the house at the southwest corner of 33rd and N Streets, a plaque reads: "In the cold winter of 1960–61 this house had an important role in history. From it was flashed to the world news of pre-inaugural announcements by President John F. Kennedy. Presented by the grateful newsmen who were given warm haven here by Miss Helen Montgomery and her father, Charles Montgomery."

Kennedy, of course, never returned to live in this house. After his assassination, the former First Lady and her children first stayed in Averell and Pamela Harriman's house for a time, then moved to 3017 N Street. Legend has it that the press camped out once again in front of her house; in response, she was said to have taken a weekend trip to New York City and returned marveling that no one had recognized her. She and the children moved there shortly thereafter.

MARY PINCHOT MEYER

3321 N STREET

$\mathcal{M}$ary Pinchot Meyer's murder in 1964 not only set off a shock wave among her Georgetown neighbors; it began a chain of political and national-security intrigues.

The ex-wife of CIA official Cord Meyer and the sister of Ben Bradlee's second wife, Tony Pinchot, Mary lived in this house after her divorce from Meyer and painted in a studio on the Bradlees' property. On October 12, 1964, while on a walk along the C&O Canal, she was shot in the head and the heart at close range and died on the towpath. An arrest was made, but the man claimed he was innocent and was later acquitted. Meyer hadn't been sexually assaulted, nor was robbery the likely motive—her purse and wallet were found back at the house. Why she'd been murdered in broad daylight was a mystery and remains so.

It was an open secret that she had had numerous trysts with President Kennedy, whose extramarital romantic exploits were legendary but at the time not well known. It was also less than a year after Kennedy's assassination and a few weeks after the release of the Warren Commission's report on his death, and the violent murder of one of the slain president's closest friends set minds spinning all over official and living-room Washington—and some of their conspiracy theories didn't seem so far-fetched.

A few hours after the murder, Tony Bradlee got a phone call from a friend of Mary's who was on a trip in Tokyo, explaining that Mary had told her that she kept a diary, and that "if anything ever happened" to her, it should be scooped up immediately. It was in the studio. The Bradlees waited until the next day to retrieve it. When they entered the studio, they got a shock—standing in the middle of the room was James Jesus Angleton, the CIA's longtime director of

Mary Pinchot Meyer had many connections to men in high places, and she may have been murdered for what she knew not far from her home at 3321 N Street.

counterintelligence. He too had been alerted to the existence of the diary and was looking for it.

The diary can no longer be found. Those who say they've read it claim that it contains evidence that Meyer and Kennedy had had an affair, but no information as to any previously unknown circumstances behind his death. It's known that Mary was signed into the White House at least a hundred times during Kennedy's short presidency—nearly all when his wife wasn't there. She was also known to have used the then-new drug LSD, and speculation has it that she shared it with JFK.

It didn't get less weird: For years a white cross was periodically planted in the ground near the spot where Mary was killed. After about ten years without one, another cross popped up in 2008. Along with the cross, however, was a red note card with the US seal folded to envelop a photocopy of a picture of Meyer and the handwritten words "cherries in the snow."

Her murderer has never been found; the DC police have kept the case open.

LLEWELLYN THOMPSON

1512 33RD STREET

*L*lewellyn Thompson spent his career in the State Department—he served as ambassador to Austria from 1952 to 1957 and to the Soviet Union from 1957 to 1962 and again from 1967 to 1969. He was also in the Foreign Service in Sri Lanka and had other roles in Moscow.

Thompson and Charles Bohlen were referred to as President Kennedy's "great demonologists" for their firsthand experience inside the Soviet Union and with Soviet leaders; in fact, Thompson not only lived in Moscow for several years but for a short time lived with future Soviet leader Nikita Khrushchev. This knowledge came in handy during the tensest times of the entire Cold War, when the possibility of World War III—perhaps even a civilization-destroying nuclear conflict—was very real.

In 1961 the Soviet Union attempted to take control of the entire city of Berlin, an enclave that under the Potsdam Agreement had been made accessible to themselves, the United States, Great Britain, and France but was situated well within the borders of East Germany, then under Soviet domination. In June of that year, Khrushchev warned Kennedy that any attempt to keep a Western presence in Berlin would lead to war. Thompson, along with Bohlen, told Kennedy that standing up to Khrushchev would result in the Soviet leader backing down.

The resulting standoff led to the construction of the Berlin Wall that summer, and eventually to Soviet attempts to deny American entry into East Berlin. The standoff at Checkpoint Charlie in October of that year led to about eighteen hours of Soviet and American tanks staring at each other in the streets of Berlin, each with orders to fire on the other if fired upon first.

Llewellyn Thompson lived at 1512 33rd Street and helped guide President Kennedy through the Cuban Missile Crisis.

Through all this, Thompson advised Kennedy that the Soviets would never try to force the West out of Berlin. Khrushchev's threat of war, he and Bohlen said, was a bluff. Slowly, five meters at a time, each side's tanks backed off. There was no war, but the Berlin Wall stood until 1990.

On October 16, 1961, American U-2 spy planes detected Soviet nuclear missiles in Cuba, about ninety miles away from the United States, with easily enough capacity and range to strike at targets within the States. The missiles were there at the request of Cuba's Fidel Castro, upset over the attempt to overthrow him in the Bay of Pigs fiasco, and were happily provided by Khrushchev, who was set off by the detection of American missiles in Italy and Turkey. Once again, it was a matter of knowing how far to push Khrushchev, and once again Kennedy sent for Thompson, who had only left the ambassador's post a couple of months before.

If anything, this was a more serious threat to the United States than the Berlin crisis, and the question at hand was no longer whether Khrushchev would start a war but whether the United States would. In the two weeks of standoffs and calculation that followed,

three options materialized: a blockade of Cuba, to prevent more Soviet ships from delivering missiles and other matériel; an invasion of the island; or a series of air strikes to destroy the missiles and their bases, which would certainly result in the deaths of Cuban civilians and Soviet troops. Kennedy decided on an interim blockade while both sides figured out what to do. Bohlen, Thompson's fellow "demonologist," had left to take the post of ambassador to France—it was decided that holding up his departure would tip the press off that something serious was up. Thompson predicted that one Soviet ship would try to breach the blockade, but when challenged it would turn around. On October 25, that's exactly what happened.

The situation, however, continued to escalate. On October 27 an American U-2 spy plane was shot down over Cuba, killing the pilot. An American ship dropped depth charges on a Soviet nuclear submarine. The sub captain ordered the missiles armed, but he was talked down by another officer. The president's brother, Attorney General Robert F. Kennedy, said that war would come in a few days. NATO allies in Europe were warned to prepare for the worst.

Through it all, Thompson advised Kennedy that Khrushchev was putting pressure on the president for other reasons and didn't actually want a war. His advice was always to give Khrushchev a way out, to "make it as easy as possible for [Khrushchev] to back down."

In the end, a deal was reached: The Soviet missiles would be dismantled and removed; in return, the missiles in Turkey would be quietly and "voluntarily" scrapped in a few months. (As it turns out, they were nearly obsolete and slated to be removed anyway, but the Soviets may not have known that, and the Turkish government, which was dead set against this part of the proposal, almost certainly didn't know.)

It was the closest the world ever got to the climactic nuclear showdown that had been feared since the dawn of the atomic age. The solution wasn't Thompson's idea—he was against the dismantling of the Turkey missiles, Gregg Herken writes—but his basic outlook, that a deal with his former host Khrushchev could be made and a global cataclysm avoided, held sway over US-Soviet dealings for the rest of the Cold War. But the thoughts that went through Llewellyn "Tommy" Thompson's head as he walked and drove through these leafy streets after days and nights on the brink of disaster aren't known—he died in 1972—and can scarcely be imagined.

31

PHILIP JESSUP

3310 P STREET

he great treaties and agreements of international affairs are generally reached across conference room tables. But once in a while, the tides of history are set in motion by two guys in a bar. And in 1949, one of those guys was Phil Jessup, who lived here on P Street, where the cars still run over cobblestones and long-disused streetcar tracks.

Cold War communications with the Soviet Union were often an exercise in the reading of tea leaves: Divining what the Soviets were saying—and not saying—could be a frustrating challenge. Sometimes their leaders, facing the challenge at home of living up to their own propaganda, needed to speak in code and hope that their signals could be read.

In 1948 Berlin was divided into four zones—American, British, French, and Soviet—as was the country as a whole. But the city itself lay within the Soviet area of Germany, and in response to a dispute over what currency would be used in the city, the Soviets blockaded Berlin and dared the Allied powers to get supplies in. This led to the Berlin Airlift, a huge US-UK combined operation that lasted from July 1948 to May 1949.

After a rocky start, the airlift was working, and, as Walter Isaacson and Evan Thomas write, "made a mockery of the Soviet attempt to strangle the city." By the end of January 1949, Charles Bohlen, the American ambassador to Moscow, thought the Kremlin would back off, although they were unwilling and/or unable to say.

On January 31 a reporter sent a list of questions on various matters to Soviet leader Joseph Stalin—"a common fishing expedition that usually produced nothing," Isaacson and Thomas wrote. "But Stalin answered." Not only did he answer, but in response to a question

Philip Jessup started a crucial conversation about the weather that helped set in motion events that allowed for the lifting of the Soviets' Berlin blockade. He lived here at 3310 P Street.

about the continued importance of the currency disagreement, Stalin replied that the stare-down was having a damaging effect on the economic redevelopment of postwar Germany.

What he didn't say was that the currency disagreement was still a matter of utmost importance.

Bohlen leapt at the seeming opening. He instructed Philip Jessup, at the time the deputy chief of the American delegation to the United Nations, to sidle up to his Soviet counterpart, Yakov Malik, in the delegates' lounge at the United Nations building in New York. The subject? The weather.

After talking for a while, Jessup mentioned, as casually as one could mention such things, that he was curious whether Stalin's omission of any mention of the currency crisis was an accident of some kind. Malik said he would check it out. Between the slow communications of the pre-Internet days, the high stakes, and the usual Soviet intransigence, it wasn't until March 14 that Malik met with Jessup to tell him that indeed, Stalin knew what he was doing: signaling that a deal was possible.

It took another month and a half for conventional negotiations to seal the deal, but on May 5, 1949, word went out that the blockade was lifted. Between the victorious conclusion to the standoff, the success of the Marshall Plan, and the demonstration of Western unity against Soviet ambitions, Winston Churchill was moved to say, "America has saved the world." And the tradition of conducting as much high-level business over drinks as over a boardroom table had been demonstrated to be as much a staple of international relations as Georgetown life.

You'd think that kind of service, as well as having played roles at the three conferences that set up the United Nations, would be enough to qualify Jessup to be the chief US representative to the UN, or at least keep Senator Joe McCarthy from labeling Jessup a "pal of Reds." But the Wisconsin senator's campaign to eliminate the perceived threat of communists in the US government—and, not coincidentally, make himself some kind of hero in the process—wasn't satisfied. He accused Jessup of "unusual affinity for communist causes"—being against further development of the atomic bomb counted, by McCarthy's own lights—and succeeded in getting Jessup's appointment as US delegate to the UN blocked.

Jessup, a lawyer, went back to teach at Columbia University, where he had studied and had taught before World War II, until 1961, when President Kennedy picked him as the American judge on the International Court of Justice, at the Hague. He served from 1961 to 1970, then went back to teaching, mostly international law. He died in 1986 at age eighty-eight. Today, the Philip C. Jessup International Law Moot Court Competition is the preeminent competition of its kind.

FRANK WISNER

3327 P STREET

rank Wisner worked at the OSS during World War II, and after a brief postwar period in private law practice he joined the CIA, becoming the head of the agency's Office of Policy Coordination—an innocuous-sounding name for a group dedicated to propaganda, economic warfare, and what its mission statement called "preventive direct action," including "sabotage, anti-sabotage, demolition and evacuation measures" and "subversion against hostile states." The office later merged with the espionage-based Office of Special Operations to form the Directorate of Plans, with Wisner at the helm and future CIA director Richard Helms as his deputy.

Wisner was one of the architects of the clandestine operations of the CIA. Working on multiple levels with multiple methods, his office came to be known as "the Wurlitzer," and it had a mixed record of success in influencing the domestic affairs of foreign countries in the direction of US interests. His first big operation, known as Project Fiend, was intended to overthrow the Stalinist dictatorship in Albania and return King Zog to the throne; it involved the dropping of leaflets, broadcasts on Radio Free Europe, and eventually the training of ethnic Albanian militias. It was a complete failure, as were most such operations in Eastern Europe.

They had more success overthrowing regimes in Central America and especially Iran—of course, the deposing of democratically elected President Mosaddegh and installation of the oil-industry-friendly Shah Reza Pahlavi in 1953 led to enmity for the United States that continues in many quarters today. He also established Operation Mockingbird, an effort by the CIA to influence not only foreign but domestic media, including the wiretapping of at least two American reporters.

When Frank Wisner wasn't hosting Sunday Night Suppers with his wife at their 3327 P Street home, he was acting as a behind-the-scenes spy, until the pressure got to be too much.

Wisner and his wife, Polly, were among the most socially active members of the Georgetown Set, and some say that the Wisners' continued immersion in the social whirl—for all its glamour, a physically taxing way of life when it's done nearly nightly after a high-stress, full-time job—didn't help Frank, who suffered two nervous breakdowns in his life, keep an even keel.

In addition to constant party-going, the Wisners were among the founders of the Sunday Night Supper, a tradition among the Georgetown Set that saw the movers and shakers congregating at a succession of houses in the neighborhood on the servants' traditional night off to try new recipes and continue the tradition of "government as club." Joe Alsop, an occasional participant, took a look at the amounts of alcohol being consumed and dubbed it the Sunday Night Drunk.

Frank Wisner was distraught over the United States' refusal to intervene in the Hungarian uprising of 1956 against the Soviet puppet government, and his already-fragile psychological condition took a turn for the worse when Soviet tanks rolled into the country. "So much of [Frank] died then," Polly would later say. He was hospitalized for six months in 1958–59, and Allen Dulles wrote that Wisner's "principal weakness is an oversensitiveness to criticism."

In 1962 Wisner, who had already been moved to London, then back to Washington but into a job far from the front lines, retired from active duty with the CIA and spent the next few years mustering responses to criticisms of the agency's covert activities in the United States and abroad over the years. His condition continued to worsen, however, and he took his own life in October 1965. His sister, Elizabeth, later wrote to Helms, "He felt that where his ability to serve further in the organization ended, his life, in fact, was over. . . . For him, the other side of the coin was blank."

Frank Wisner was an avid gardener, and there's a plaque in his memory in the Bishop's Garden at the National Cathedral. Perhaps befitting a man who worked undercover and behind the scenes, his memorial doesn't consist of a gorgeous flower or even a sturdy shrub—it's the sprinkler system, the component that makes everything else possible.

DESMOND FITZGERALD

1641 34TH STREET

*L*ike so many others in the Georgetown Set, Desmond FitzGerald returned from World War II to his New York law firm only to find that that life simply didn't hold the same appeal that it had before the war. Having worked as a liaison officer with a Chinese unit in Burma, he had eaten monkey brains in the jungle and debated the best techniques for getting rid of a Chinese ghost. Wall Street didn't stand a chance.

FitzGerald began his career at the Office of Policy Coordination, a forerunner of the CIA, in 1950, returning to Burma during the Korean War and overseeing a disastrous campaign to fund and arm Chinese nationalist soldiers to fight against Chinese communists pursuing the retreating General Douglas MacArthur. He became Far East chief at the CIA in 1958, taking on the job of raising, training, and funding secret armies in Laos, Tibet, the Philippines, and Thailand in order to stop communist uprisings, and to overthrow governments and install regimes favorable to the United States.

"We are not here to monitor communism," FitzGerald once famously told a friend; "we are here to destroy it." He would recruit spies and guerillas and set up political parties and other organizations that were really front groups for US and CIA interests, as well as other CIA operatives to do the same, ending up elbow-deep in some of the more bloody and less legal battles of the Cold War. It was said that his ideal agent would be a Harvard PhD who could also win a bar fight (not a bad description of himself), but if he couldn't get both qualities, he'd settle for one or the other.

Most famously, FitzGerald was brought back to Washington in 1963 to manage the plot first to overthrow, then to assassinate, Cuba's Fidel Castro. Under orders from Robert F. Kennedy, the president's

Desmond FitzGerald lived here at 1641 34th Street while chief of the CIA's clandestine operations. His daughter, Frances FitzGerald, is a Pulitzer Prize-winning author for her book on Vietnam, Fire in the Lake.

brother and US attorney general, FitzGerald recruited Cuban agents of the CIA to blow up Cuban mines and other infrastructure, only to fail at the cost of twenty-five lives. He was then ordered to find a way to do away with Castro once and for all, giving the job to a CIA source in the Cuban government. Not only was the attempt a failure, it was also suggested, not without some logic, that the would-be hit man was in fact a double agent and had tipped Castro to the plot, and that the assassination of President Kennedy just a few weeks later was a Cuban plot in retribution.

After that, FitzGerald took on the innocuous-sounding title of deputy director for plans—chief of the CIA's clandestine operations. He worked all over the world, including in the undercover fight against communism in Vietnam. Outwardly supportive of the fight against North Vietnamese leader Ho Chi Minh, he argued that a "hearts and minds" campaign of overt and covert political action in the south would do more than a military campaign. After the twin disasters of the Bay of Pigs and the Castro plot, however, the CIA wasn't very well trusted in the Johnson administration. William Colby, who succeeded FitzGerald as Far East director, said, "The communists were fighting a people's war and here we were putting in divisions. After the Bay of Pigs we turned the war over to the military and they just screwed it up."

FitzGerald already wasn't exactly the typical Georgetown homeowner, and the trials of the mid-sixties took a toll on him. A product of the Ivy League like so many of his compatriots, he was described as a genteel sort, with a demeanor more befitting an English gentleman of long ago. He was said by his coworkers to run his department with the élan of a real-life James Bond—he was known for frequently quoting from *Alice's Adventures in Wonderland* during meetings to illustrate a point—but would also fall into gloom, once writing to his daughter, "I must say that the world is a dark and dangerous place and the dehumanization of man has made terrible progress."

None of this helped his family life: His stepdaughter once recalled her mother complaining about the household staff, only to have FitzGerald cut her off by saying, "Do you realize that I have four men on a hill in China with very little hope of getting them back?" Another stepdaughter said of her mother, "She couldn't very well say, 'How did your meeting with the spy go, dear? Did you snuff him?'"

When he wasn't morose or stressed, he could be closed-off or bizarre—he once surprised his family in the car on the way home from an outing by suggesting, "Let's have a talk." The talk turned out to consist of FitzGerald holding forth for an hour on the workings of the internal combustion engine.

In January 1967 the left-wing magazine *Ramparts* blew the whistle on CIA front groups around the world and, most unsettlingly, in the United States, where it was expressly forbidden to operate. In the spring of that year, the Castro assassination plot was made public. FitzGerald was soon besieged by investigators asking questions about the plot and its possible ramifications against the Kennedys; added to this was James Angleton's constant molehunt, a worsening situation in Vietnam, and the growing sense that no one was listening to him. "The pressure of the job [of running the clandestine service] got to him," a CIA official said.

On one of the DC area's infamously hot and humid days in July 1967, FitzGerald and his wife, Barbara (his second wife; he divorced shortly after World War II), played mixed doubles against the British ambassador and his wife. Slathered in lotion to protect his skin, which had developed a permanent sensitivity to the sun in Burma, FitzGerald tossed the ball up to serve, keeled over from a heart attack, and died. He was fifty-six.

CIA agent Archie Roosevelt later said that when Desmond Fitz-Gerald became chief of the clandestine service, "The whole place was charged with dynamism. . . . Now, the fun is gone."

34

WALTER LIPPMANN
1525 35TH STREET

The term "Cold War" is so universally known that it's hard to imagine that someone actually coined it, but Walter Lippmann did, using it as the title of his 1947 book. Even if he hadn't, his place at the center of twentieth-century thinking about the United States' role in the world had already been assured.

Lippmann, along with the Alsop brothers, was among the journalists whom the Truman administration, and George Kennan and Dean Acheson specifically, reached out to for help selling the American public on the importance of rebuilding postwar Europe through what came to be known as the Marshall Plan—not just through a sense of altruism, but for the purpose of saving Europe from Soviet economic predation. Later, Lippmann, Joe Alsop, the *New York Times*'s James Reston (who lived in the Cathedral Heights area), and the *Washington Post*'s Phil Graham were the four journalists whose calls President Kennedy ordered should be put through to the Oval Office immediately.

Lippmann was one of the cofounders of *The New Republic* in 1914, and during World War I worked in a propaganda office. His first brush with history came when he helped write Woodrow Wilson's Fourteen Points, which documented the United States' goals in getting involved in World War I—an influential document that laid out an essentially moral case for war, something every American intervention in a foreign conflict has felt the need to do since.

While Lippmann practiced journalism, he also wrote about and influenced it—in some people's minds, he created what we think of as journalism today. After the war, Lippmann began his newspaper column, which continued for nearly fifty years, and wrote three books on what he'd learned about the molding of public opinion and the power that the press held to enlighten, or benight, their readers.

Walter Lippmann was a Pulitzer Prize–winning journalist and political commentator who held famous salons at his Georgetown home at 1525 35th Street.

When journalists "arrogate to themselves the right to determine by their own consciences what shall be reported and for what purpose," Lippmann wrote, "democracy is unworkable. Public opinion is blockaded. For when a people can no longer confidently repair 'to the best foundations for their information,' then anyone's guess and anyone's rumor, each man's hope and each man's whim becomes the basis of government. . . . No one can manage anything on pap. Neither can a people."

Lippmann's column, Today and Tomorrow, alternated with Joseph and Stewart Alsop's Matter of Fact column in the *New York Herald Tribune*, *Washington Post*, and, presumably, the papers both columns were syndicated to nationwide. Millions of readers across the country, then, got an alternating view of the world every workday.

Joe Alsop considered himself and Lippmann simultaneously friends and rivals. "Lippmann was in a world of his own, and it was a world that Joe envied," a reporter who knew them both once said. While Alsop had no small amount of political pull, Lippmann was a better known and more respected commentator on the national scene—which evidently grated on Alsop. Lippmann was less comfortable with, and less optimistic about, the idea of using American military force around the world; Alsop found Lippmann's views unserious and naive. (Lippmann also won two Pulitzer Prizes; Alsop never won one.)

Walter Lippmann was no slouch as a social host either, but again, his and Alsop's styles were opposites. While Lippmann's parties and dinners were attended by many of the same outspoken dignitaries who verbally brawled at Joe Alsop's house, Lippmann's wasn't the place for that. Robert Merry writes, "Lippmann, ever the diplomat, found raucous social debates distasteful. At his famous Georgetown salon, whenever he detected temperatures rising at table, he would deftly change the subject to calm the situation. He fostered sedate, learned discussions not just on Washington politics but also on literature and art and goings-on at Whitehall in London or the Elysée in Paris."

The last great public campaign of Lippmann's life was his opposition to the Vietnam War, although he once warned of the futility of the war using the same casual racism that some American military leaders used as the basis of their explanations for lack of progress:

The Vietnamese, he wrote, "do not value their material possessions, which are few, nor even their lives, which are short and unhappy, as do the people of a country who have much to lose and much to live for." President Johnson was reportedly outraged by Lippmann's opposition to the war, and it was later discovered that a White House team had been tasked with assembling a dossier of Lippmann's previous work to show that he was a habitual peacenik.

The alternation of the Alsops' column and Lippmann's was particularly noticeable during the mid-1960s, when the subject was Vietnam. Gregg Herken writes, "On Mondays, Wednesdays, and Fridays, Alsop's Matter of Fact column declared confidently that the war was being won and 'standing fast is paying off.' On Tuesdays and Thursdays, Lippmann's Today and Tomorrow urged the president to halt the bombing and seek a negotiated peace."

Lippmann retired, in part because of the stress caused by his hassles with the Johnson White House, and moved to New York in 1967. Alsop, despite his conflicts with Lippmann and the opening up of the unofficial slot of dean of Washington journalists (which Alsop claimed he now filled), wrote to Lippmann and his wife, Helen, "I miss you sadly, on Tuesday and Thursday, and the whole city will always miss both of you." Lippmann died in 1974.

35

DAVID AND EVANGELINE BRUCE
1405 34TH STREET

When it came to foreign relations, David Bruce worked both ends of the street, in the OSS as "Wild Bill" Donovan's right-hand man during World War II, and in aboveboard diplomacy as ambassador to France (1949–52), West Germany (1957–59), and England (1961–69), and the United States' first emissary to China (1973–74), as well as undersecretary of state. His first wife was a Mellon heiress. He was a doughboy in World War I, and hung out with Ernest Hemingway during World War II. His biography is titled *The Last American Aristocrat*, and his life's story is the stuff of an epic film.

Bruce's second wife, Evangeline, was an integral part of the Georgetown social scene. Every morning at nine, she, Polly Wisner, and Kay Graham would have a three-way phone conversation that Phil Graham called the "nine o'clock network" and added that he wanted in. On many Monday afternoons, the three would take part in an informal cooking class run by Julia Child, a former OSS clerk who had a way in the kitchen.

David Bruce called his wife his "secret weapon." Her ease with French culture and the French language charmed the country when her husband was ambassador there, and her ability to deal with the social obligations of being an ambassador's wife was legendary. While many referred to her as a brilliant hostess, she didn't like the term: "What I do is run the social wing of the embassy," she once said. "I entertain. I organize. That doesn't make me a hostess. There's a difference."

She added that there was serious business behind what she did: She compared entertaining to being an architect, saying, "You must design and structure a setting in which deals can be made and information exchanged."

David and Evangeline Bruce were legendary hosts, whether throwing parties here at their Georgetown residence at 1405 34th Street or hosting soirees abroad.

It wasn't all smooth sailing. The Bruces had three children. Their eldest, Sasha, died in 1975 after a short marriage to a man who stole from the family, admitted hitting her, and fled to his native Greece ahead of police questioning. The matter of whether her death was a suicide or a murder has never been fully resolved.

"One was so proud as an American," Jacqueline Kennedy Onassis once wrote to Evangeline, "to think that other countries recognized you as our very best."

36

JAMES FORRESTAL
3508 PROSPECT STREET

There wasn't a lot of shooting in the Cold War, but there were plenty of victims.

James Forrestal, born in 1892 in New York State, graduated from Princeton University, was a navy pilot in World War I, and made a fortune on Wall Street afterward. Active in the Democratic Party, he helped candidates including Franklin Delano Roosevelt, who in 1940 made him undersecretary of the navy and, in 1944, secretary.

Forrestal was focused on defeating the Germans and Japanese, of course, but he was also one of a group of Americans who also saw some kind of conflict with the Soviet Union coming up after the present war was over. And when Harry Truman ascended to the presidency, Forrestal had a willing ear. In 1946 Forrestal was a champion of George Kennan and of the philosophy expressed in Kennan's "Long Telegram"—that a full-on shooting war with the Soviet Union was unnecessary but that friendship and cooperation was impossible, not least because the Soviet government needed to unite its people behind a common enemy.

In 1947 Truman named Forrestal the secretary of defense. Forrestal wrote that "this office will probably be the greatest cemetery for dead cats in history," but he began to advocate for two of his lifelong positions: First, he established racial integration across all US armed forces, as he had already done in the navy. Second, he took on communism in two ways—overtly as one of the architects of the Marshall Plan, under which American money would rebuild war-destroyed Europe (and make and cement friends along the way), and covertly with the creation of what would become the CIA.

Forrestal approved of Kennan's plan for a "guerrilla warfare corps" to carry out operations whose scope and means the American

As secretary of defense under President Truman, James Forrestal established integration across all US armed forces and created what would become the CIA. He lived at 3508 Prospect Street.

people and their representatives might not appreciate had they known about them. With Allen Dulles, he went about raising the money for a clandestine service, hustling donations and setting up transfers from various funds, including Marshall Plan money.

But Forrestal's job, and the feeling that he was one of a handful of lonely sentinels on the watch against the Soviet menace, was wearing on him. He was secretary of defense at a time when the mandate was to reduce defense spending, scrap weapons, and generally take the nation off a war footing. Forrestal felt this was an abdication of his responsibilities, and this conflict tore at him. He began to sleep in his office, develop nervous tics, and act strangely.

Forrestal sided with the Joint Chiefs of Staff, who wanted more military spending, and against the president, who demanded less. The last straw came when Drew Pearson reported that Forrestal had met with Thomas Dewey, Truman's opponent in the 1948 election, to discuss his staying on if, as was expected, Dewey won. (Consider the source: Pearson published many pieces critical of Forrestal, at least two of which were demonstrably false.) Truman was reelected in an upset, and Forrestal was fired in March 1949.

"During his last day in office," Tim Weiner writes in his history of the CIA, "he broke down, moaning that he had not slept in months." Forrestal was committed to the National Naval Medical Center (now the Walter Reed National Military Medical Center) in Bethesda, Maryland. In the early hours of May 22, 1949, his body was found on a third-floor roof below his sixteenth-floor room. He was fifty-seven.

His death was ruled a suicide. Theories as to unreported causes of his demise abound: The Soviets got to him, some say; others think the Zionists got to him (he was considered an opponent of Israel, although many consider those accusations a stretch at best). Weiner writes that Forrestal spent his last night copying lines from the chorus of Sophocles' play *Ajax*, and that his final written word was "night —": that he had begun to write "nightingale" but stopped in the middle and leapt from a window. Nightingale, Weiner writes, was the code name for a covert army Forrestal had set up under the auspices of the CIA that included former Nazi-collaborationist murderers. One conspiracy theorist points out—correctly—that the handwriting on the paper purportedly found in Forrestal's room bears no resemblance to known samples of his writing.

The only thing that's absolutely verified is the pain he was feeling.

Forrestal's son Michael was a defense aide to President Kennedy. James Forrestal's name adorns a building at Princeton, a building in Washington now used as the headquarters of the US Department of Energy, and the United States' first supercarrier, one of the largest warships ever built, which served for nearly forty years. The ship's slogan was "First in Defense."

Georgetown's historic cobblestone streets include streetcar tracks from the old Metropolitan Railroad.

CONCLUSION

There's still no shortage of powerful people living in Georgetown: Secretary of State John Kerry lives at 3322 O Street and former secretary of state Madeleine Albright lives at 1318 34th Street in a house formerly lived in by Lorraine Shevlin, who later married John Sherman Cooper, a Republican senator from Kentucky, former ambassador to East Germany and India, and the host of John F. Kennedy's first dinner party as president. But the kind of concentration of governmental, bureaucratic, diplomatic, and journalistic power in Georgetown that the 1960s and 1970s saw—and the informal-yet-serious discussions that happened at the parties there—are now mostly history.

But the houses remain; the streets remain; the buckling brick sidewalks remain. Stewart Alsop once wrote that "Washington's May makes up for Washington's August, which is saying a great deal," and it's especially in those uniquely glorious springs and sweltering summers, especially when the sidewalks are relatively empty, a certain sense that Stewart Alsop wrote about decades ago is still in the air:

> [T]he gossip, the jokes, the predictions about who is going to get whose job, the stories about some awful thing the President said to an amazed lady the other night, the head-counting before a major vote, the freewheeling argument on the issues . . .
>
> It is good, too, to live in the midst of great events, to live in history—even as an onlooker, a mere provider of footnotes.

The onlookers and the actors not only lived in Georgetown; in a real sense they worked there. To walk in their footsteps helps us understand who the Georgetown Set were, what they did, and under what remarkable circumstances they did it.